FORTUNE-TELLING BY TAROT CARDS

A practical guide containing all you need to know to look into the
future using your Tarot cards.

D0380512

FORTUNE-TELLING BY TAROT CARDS

A Beginner's Guide to Understanding the Future Using Tarot Cards

by

SASHA FENTON

THE AQUARIAN PRESS
Wellingborough, Northamptonshire

First published 1985

8   10   12   14   15   13   11   9

British Library Cataloguing in Publication Data

Fenton, Sasha
    Fortune-telling by tarot cards
    1. Tarot
    I. Title
    133.3'2424   BF1879.T2

    ISBN 0-85030-445-8

*The Aquarian Press is part of the
Thorsons Publishing Group*

Printed and bound in Great Britain

Dedication

This book is dedicated to my family:
my husband, Tony;
my children, Helen and Stuart;
my parents, Frances and Sam Waxman.

Acknowledgements

Grateful thanks to Les Friend
who introduced me to the Tarot all those years ago.

CONTENTS

PREFACE

The cards which have been used to illustrate this book are brand new. They were first conceived as a project in 1981 by the Tarot Consultant and Psychic Researcher, Bernard Stringer. It took him over a year and a half to find the artist, Peter Richardson, with whom he could share his inspiration and communicate his experience of the Tarot into images of beauty. Peter Richardson's translation of Bernard Stringer's ideas bring a new dimension to the visual images. The chosen symbolism has been interwoven with care and precision thereby adding clarity of meaning to the cards.

Bernard Stringer considers that the preparation of the 'Prediction Tarot' has been an exciting journey in which both he and Peter Richardson hoped to achieve something which was lacking in most other cards; namely the feeling of a living card. The pictures on the cards will be instantly recognizable to experienced Tarot Readers because they are derived from familiar historical sources. The portrayals place these most modern of cards firmly in the ancestral gallery of Tarot history. They both hope that the strength and the beauty of the images on the 'Prediction Tarot' will bring a greater level of understanding to both experienced and novice Tarot users.

My own introduction to this deck of cards was in a particularly 'pure' form as I saw the original paintings by Peter Richardson from which the cards have now been produced. I loved their 'wintery' colours and precise detail. They have a strongly 'masculine' feel about them which hauntingly expresses Man's continuing desire to understand the universe and the need to tap into hidden power sources of higher consciousness. The eternal need to find meaning in the mysteries of life and death.

On another level there is tremendous sensuality expressed in these cards. Which woman could fail to fall in love with the young man on the Lovers card (VI). Which man could resist the fabulous Star of Hope (XVII). The Hanged Man (XII) looks so uncomfortable suspended between his past and his present, he would feel so much better if only someone gave him the initiative to release himself. The royal household of Emperor (IIII) and Empress (III) remind us of what we could achieve if we put our minds to it, and of the material things we could enjoy as a result of endeavour.

The court cards with their serious purposeful faces deal with our day-to-day obligations, our messages, journeys and business matters. They also remind us of our need to associate and communicate with others and, of course, of our commitments to those who depend upon us. The Hierophant (V), Priestess (II) and the Hermit (VIIII) require us to rise above mere materialism, to study and reflect and also of our obligations of charity and mercy to others. The Judgement card (XX) and the World (XXI) take us through even as far as the completion of our earthly lives, and remind us that we will enter a new world one day which has its own Halls of Learning and which will offer us many adventures in other places even after we leave here.

SASHA FENTON

INTRODUCTION

There is a great deal of interest in the occult these days and in all forms of fortune-telling. It is quite the thing to own a pack of Tarot cards and better still, to be able to use them. There are books which are supposed to tell you how to read the Tarot, but not one of them gives really clear and simple instructions in everyday English which a complete beginner can understand.

Tarot cards are a popular present, all of them are sold with an instruction leaflet or booklet. These instructions tend to be terribly confusing, contradictory and are often far too brief. I have written this book for people who want to understand the cards on a practical down-to-earth level. I do not rule out the use of the cards for the purposes of meditation, greater enlightenment, or as a religious experience, but in this book I only seek to help the novice reader to enjoy and make use of their pack of Tarot cards.

I have given descriptions and illustrations of a number of different layouts in this book, the student Reader can try them out and later on perhaps invent some for himself. The pictures on the Major Arcana send out such powerful visual messages that after a short while the reader will find his or her own meanings for the cards. However, even the most experienced readers are short of an idea from time to time, therefore I have made a précis of both the Major Arcana and Minor Arcana sections which can be used to jog the memory. This is the kind of book that should be kept near the cards as a handy reference guide.

The Origins of the Tarot

Nobody knows for certain where Tarot cards originally came from but they seem to share the same roots as playing cards and the game of chess. There are claims put forward that China, India or Egypt is the birthplace of the Tarot, I feel sure that influences from all these places, and a good many more, have been drawn on by the early card designers. It is probable that the packs which finally emerged, more or less in their present form, in the fourteenth century were developed from those which were carried by travelling people and gypsies during their periodic westerly migrations.

An early card game which was called 'Tarocco' in Italy and 'Tarot' in France used the now familiar format of four suits of cards numbered from Ace to 10 with figures of King, Queen, Cavalier and Page. The suits were in the familiar form of Cups, Staves (Rods or Wands), Swords and Coins (or Pentacles) – although the names changed slightly from one country to another, or even from one area to another. This game actually used the 22 Major Arcana cards which were used as trump cards; the only one which still remains in playing card packs is the Fool which is now called the Joker.

There is an account of cards being used for fortune-telling in the fourteenth century French court, when a gypsy was brought in to entertain the King. She was able to describe intimate details of the people around him and tell him of future events with such accuracy that fortune-telling by cards became tremendously popular. So much so that the King became thoroughly fed-up with it and banned the cards from the court altogether.

Since then, Tarot cards have gone through a number of phases of popularity and banishment over the years, and are at the moment once more extremely popular. The image that they have of being slightly dangerous in some unspecified way, only serves to increase their attraction. In actual fact, Tarot cards are not in the least dangerous as they rely upon the intuition, and possible psychic powers of the reader and in no way release dangerous or frightening forces. If the reader treats them with respect but does not worry too much about any one particular reading, then they can be entertaining, informative and a useful guide to future actions.

1

RITUAL AND PROCEDURE

Looking After the Cards

Tarot cards which are meant to be used for divination should not be used for card games. They should be kept either in their box or in a drawstring bag. Many professional readers like to wrap their cards in a silk scarf to insulate the cards from outside influences. I have never done this, I just keep them in their box. The cards should be used only by you, the Reader, except when being shuffled by the Questioner prior to a reading. Other people should not be allowed to mess about with them or they will pick up too many cross-vibrations.

New Cards

It is a good idea to 'work up' a new pack by laying each card on top of the same card from an old deck. If you have no old deck of your own, then be careful whose deck you use for this. If this idea does not appeal to you, then just keep on shuffling the cards and doing some test readings for yourself and your family until they lose their newness.

Guidelines for Readers

Always be careful not to frighten a Questioner when you are giving a reading. Most people tend to take what is said to them very seriously, even if they are outwardly sceptical or even derisory. It would be unforgivable to frighten or upset someone needlessly. Even a very experienced professional Reader has to take care when giving bad news, but in the case of an absolute beginner, if your Questioner should happen to pick out a set of really black cards, I would actually advise you to tone your interpretation right down, even to the point of risking your credibility. If you maintain your interest in the Tarot, you will soon learn to judge people and develop an instinct for giving bad news tactfully but confidently.

People are funny; the majority of us are quite happy to be gently criticized by a Reader, we also enjoy being told that we have had a lot to put up with in the past (who hasn't?). We don't even mind being told that we will have to face a few more problems in the future, but we really hate to hear of specific health problems, troubles affecting our children, or that a loved one is being unfaithful. So as a Reader, even if you are absolutely convinced that the Questioner sitting in front of you has a youngster who will soon be in trouble with the law, a spouse who is putting it about and a really majestic cancer growing right in the middle of his middle -- do yourself a favour, tone it all down a little!

Dealing the Cards

When you are ready to try a reading, sit somewhere quiet and comfortable. Use a table which is large enough to spread the cards out on; the dining table is often a popular place for this. Shuffle the cards a little if you wish, then pass them on to the Questioner and let him or her give them a good shuffle. Ask the Questioner to cut the cards into three decks, using the left hand (nearest to the heart). If you wish to give an upright and reversed reading, you can also ask the Questioner to choose one of the three decks which you can then turn round. The Questioner should then put all the cards back together again in any order he or she prefers. Then you should pick up the cards so that the end that pointed towards the Questioner now points towards you. Now you are ready to begin.

For a reading using upright and reversed cards
The Questioner cuts the cards into three decks
and then chooses one of them.

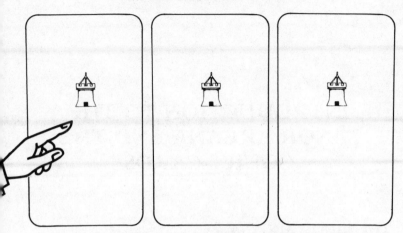

The Reader turns the deck which the Questioner has chosen.

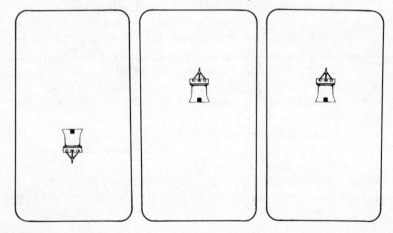

The end which was nearest to the Questioner must be placed nearest
to the Reader.

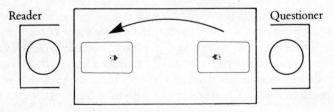

2

INTRODUCTION TO THE MINOR ARCANA AND THE COURT CARDS

THE MINOR ARCANA

The Minor Arcana of the Tarot is composed of four suits of cards, these are Cups, Staves (Rods or Wands), Swords and Coins (or Pentacles). Each of these suits have numbered cards from Ace to 10, plus four court cards which are the Page, Knight, Queen and King. In some European countries, the Minor Arcana cards are still actually used as playing cards. Some of the packs which are meant for card games have heads at both ends in the same way that our playing cards do.

It is just about feasible for someone to give a reading by means of the Minor Arcana only – after all there are many skilled playing card readers around, but it usual for both the Major and the Minor Arcana cards to be used together. A good many readers like to give a reading using just the Major Arcana first, then another reading using the complete pack.

THE COURT CARDS

The court cards cause quite a lot of confusion for those wishing to learn the Tarot as they *may* represent actual people who are already in the Questioner's environment or who may yet come into his life. The court cards may also represent situations and events rather than actual persons in the Questioner's life, or they may be people to meet and deal with who will leave no great or lasting impression on the Questioner but who may spark off events and turning points as they pass by. There is also the fraught question of how to identify specific people in the subject's life from the court cards – even the simple act of choosing a Significator* to represent the Questioner is filled with problems. So let us try to analyse and deal with these questions in a fairly logical manner.

Choosing a Significator

The Gipsy Method
In earlier times, before the advent of television and radio, people were forced to find ways to entertain themselves in order to combat boredom. We have all heard about the singsongs around the piano that people supposedly enjoyed in the old days, haven't we? Well, among other things, fortune-telling was a much more popular pastime than it is today, and one could almost guarantee that in every family there would be an old auntie somewhere who had a 'way' with tea leaves or playing cards. The usual method of telling fortunes by means of playing cards was to allocate certain categories of age and general appearance to each of the court cards, and this is still used by many readers today, both by means of Tarot cards and ordinary playing cards. The following analysis will demonstrate the method.

Kings   – These are mature men of at least 35 years of age, possibly older.

Queens – These are mature adult women.

Knights – These are young adult men.

Pages   – These are children and young people of both sexes.

Cups   – Blonde haired, light skinned people.

Staves   – Brown haired, light skinned people.

Swords – Dark complexioned, dark haired people.

Coins   – Very dark complexioned, dark haired people.

If the reader wants to use ordinary playing cards they can be treated as follows:

   Combine the Knight and Page cards to make the Jack; i.e. young or immature persons of either sex.

*The Significator is a card which has been chosen by the Reader to represent the Questioner.

Cups are like Hearts
Staves are like Clubs
Swords are like Spades
Coins are like Diamonds

In fact our familiar playing cards developed from the same source as the Minor Arcana of the Tarot. One can see an immediate correlation between Staves and Clubs. The Diamond probably got its name from its shape – remember the Coins are often called Pentacles because of the five pointed star on each coin in some packs. The Hearts are harder to find an explanation for, but it might again stem from the shape of the Cups or the designs on them on some of the ancient packs. The name 'Spade' is a corruption of 'Espada' which is Spanish for Sword!

The Astrological Method
This method is based on astrology with the theory being that the four suits relate to the four astrological elements, and therefore to the signs of the zodiac.

Cups   – Water signs, i.e. Cancer, Scorpio and Pisces.

Staves   – Air signs, i.e. Gemini, Libra and Aquarius.
          Or Fire signs, i.e. Aries, Leo and Sagittarius.

Swords   – Air signs, i.e. Gemini, Libra and Aquarius.
          Or Fire signs, i.e. Aries, Leo and Sagittarius.

Coins   – Earth signs, i.e. Taurus, Virgo and Capricorn.

As you can see, Tarot readers cannot agree about the Air and Fire signs and this is in my opinion a particularly awkward method of interpretation.

The way a Court Card might be used goes something like this. Say, for instance, the King of Swords was prominent in the layout, the Reader might say to the Questioner 'you are going to have a significant meeting with someone born under the sign of Gemini, Libra or Aquarius (*or* Aries, Leo or Sagittarius)'. I personally have never really felt at home with this method, but that is not in any way to disparage those who get good results by using it. In many ways this dilemma isolates the chief problem with regard to the Tarot (or any other form of interpretative work), that every Reader or potential Reader must find out what works for him or her and must not necessarily follow a rigid pattern. Any book on the Tarot can only give guidelines and the Reader must find his own way to success by trial, error and practice. *This is a most important point.*

Other Popular Ideas
Some Readers associate particular professions with particular cards such as a doctor or lawyer for the King of Swords or a business woman for the Queen of Staves. The booklets which come with the packs of cards when one buys them often mention such things as 'A man, kindly disposed to the Questioner, who lives in the country'. All this is fair enough but is not really sufficiently flexible.

Sasha's Method
This really is a mixture of all the other methods. First of all, if I happen to be using a Significator to represent the Questioner, I will choose one to fit his appearance and what little I may know of his nature. Therefore, I may choose the Queen of Staves for a chatty working woman with medium colouring, and the King of Coins for a steady, quiet, down-to-earth (if not an actual earth sign), darkish haired man.

Kings and Queens, on the whole, are actual people who are now, or shortly will be, a part of the Questioner's life. The Reader should always use his or her own intuition with regard to the type of person any court card represents. If my description does not *feel* right, then by all means change it. My interpretations are tried and tested, but nevertheless time and practice will show the Reader the type of person each court card represents to him or her.

Knights, of course, can represent people, and in general the colouring and the behaviour of these people is rather like that of the King's, but possibly in a watered down form. Another curious thing about the Knights is that they may actually represent a mature person – the type who would normally be represented by the King, but this person may be diminishing in importance to the Questioner in the future. For instance, a person who has had a central and significant effect on the Questioner in recent years will either shortly move away, or for some other reason, just become less important (either for good or ill) to the Questioner. I call this the 'law of diminishing persons' and it is quite strange how it seems to work. The former star performer in our Questioner's life may reduce from a King, to a Knight and then to a Page before disappearing completely out of his or her sphere of interest. This 'diminishing' situation may be temporary or permanent, a glance at other cards in the spread may help the Reader here. It is also worth noting that this kind of situation requires fairly frequent readings and a Questioner who already knows which card signifies whom in his life.

Pages are often children or very youthful people. Generally speaking, the Page of Cups and Coins will be fairly steady and peaceful children while the Pages of Staves and Swords signify the more active type of child. The colouring of the child is blonde for Cups, brown for Staves, darkish for Swords and very dark for Coins.

If more than one Page appears in a spread, then children are in the forefront of the Questioner's mind, or there may just be a lot of documentation, telephone calls, letters and general communications on the way to the Questioner. There may be scandal or gossip, mixed up communications and misunderstandings, especially if the Pages are reversed.

So to sum up the Court cards; it is generally assumed that a King represents a lover, husband, boss, authority figure, father, brother or friend. A Queen represent a lover, wife, boss, mother, sister or friend. A Knight represents a lover, friend, brother (or sister) or a colleague. A Page represents a child, friend or messenger. However, these people may not even stay for very long in the Questioner's life and the cards will show the *impact* that the character has on the Questioner at the time of the reading and this may be the impact of a situation rather than a person.

3
THE SUIT OF CUPS

The suit of Cups is associated with romance, marriage and material goods and possessions. Cups also indicate warmth and friendship, partnerships and even the kind of affection a person may have for their pet! Educational matters and the visual arts are also associated with Cup cards.

Ace of Cups

Meaning

The beginning of an affectionate loving or friendly association for the questioner. At best this may be the romance of a lifetime, or a marriage made in heaven, at the very least it indicates new friendships, good social life and good companionship. It also may indicate that a gift is coming to the questioner, often a ring – even a wedding ring! A birth is also possible.

Reversed Meaning

This gives a watered down version of the upright Ace. Therefore, affection rather than outright *love* could be on the way to the Questioner, or more sadly someone who did love the Questioner could be losing interest at the time of the reading.

Two of Cups

Meaning
A partnership. This may be romantic or to do with business. Therefore if the Questioner has just met somebody interesting, this card would indicate that a romance will blossom. Even if this is a business partnership, there will be a liking and friendship for the people involved – whatever sex they may be. It can also mean two people making up after an argument or getting engaged, or making a commitment to each other.

Reversed Meaning
This reverses the above reading. There will be a parting which might be temporary and due to unforseen circumstances or there may be a complete split in the relationship. Other cards in the reading will help to clarify matters. It is possible that the desired relationship will not get off the ground in the first place.

Three of Cups

Meaning
This is a fun card which shows up when pleasant celebrations are due to occur. There might be a wedding for the Questioner soon, or he may officiate at somebody else's wedding. There may be the birth of a child, a house-warming or any reason for a celebration.

Reversed Meaning
A confusing card, it may indicate fun, frivolity and sex, however, it can show that an expected or hoped for marriage will not take place. There may even be a divorce, or it could indicate that an affair which is taking place will not turn into marriage later on.

Four of Cups

Meaning
This is a peculiar card as it shows dissatisfaction. It shows that the
Questioner has advantages under his nose which he cannot see,
but wants something which he does not have, or even does not
really know what it is that he wants. Perhaps the grass is greener on
the other side of the hill.

Reversed Meaning
The meaning of the upright card is reversed here. The Questioner
makes up his mind as to what it is that he wants, or decides to make
the best of what he already has. Also new friends and experiences
are on the way.

Five of Cups

Meaning

This is a miserable card which shows loss and sadness. However, this is not total loss, there is definitely something left to look forward to, whatever has been lost, there is still something left from which to begin to build for the future. There is a sense of looking back with regret, possibly even some kind of mourning.

Reversed Meaning

A sense of loss and a period of unhappiness is passing away and there will be good times again in the future, possibly meeting up with old friends again.

Six of Cups

Meaning
This card shows a need to reach back into the past in order to build for the future. Therefore, the Questioner should go back to his roots in some way, either by using some old skill or experience or by getting in touch with old friends and family contacts. It often comes up just before a happy family gathering.

Reversed Meaning
This reverses the meaning of the upright card. It can indicate that a planned family get-together will be a disaster, or that the answer to the Questioner's problems does not lie in the past but will require a new outlook on life. The family are not likely to help and perhaps it is time to admit to personal mistakes and *grow up*.

Seven of Cups

Meaning
This card shows confusion. There are too many roads to choose
from and some of them will be dead ends. Perhaps it is best for the
Questioner to coast along for a while rather than trying to make
far reaching decisions at this time. If money is a stumbling block in
a romance, this should soon be sorted out.

Reversed Meaning
Muddles and indecision will soon sort themselves out.

Eight of Cups

Meaning
There is a miserable situation involving the Questioner just now, but there *is* light at the end of the tunnel. The message is to be courageous and patient, things will work out eventually. It is possible that a blonde woman will change the Questioner's life in some way soon.

Reversed Meaning
A definite end to a rotten situation is now in view. There should be some joy and fun ahead.

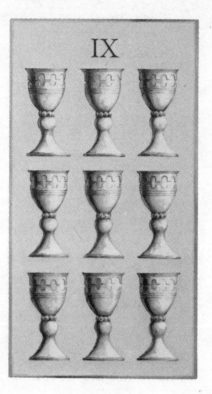

Nine of Cups

Meaning

This card shows that the Questioner is (or soon will be) very pleased with himself. This is fine as long as he remembers not to appear too smug to less fortunate people. Marriage to a mature type of person may be on the way.

Reversed Meaning

Not a bad card as it shows some satisfaction to come, but there may still be a slight touch of irritation. If, for instance, the Questioner failed in an exam, he would not have failed by a great margin and would be advised to try again. Any problems should be sorted out soon.

Ten of Cups

Meaning
This is sometimes called the 'wish' card, if this shows up in a reading, the Questioner can expect to get all that he desires.

Reversed Meaning
This may be a watered down version of the upright card, i.e. partial success in obtaining one's desires, but it may be that someone else will be getting a fair bit of the Questioner's share of the spoils. There may be arguments in a relationship or within the family. A complete split up is possible. A look at other cards nearby will give some more clues about this one.

PAGE OF CUPS

Page of Cups

Meaning

A loving gentle youngster, possibly blonde with fair colouring.

Often the Pages are not people but situations. The Page of Cups indicates a time to think and study and possibly the passing of exams. It often shows up before the Questioner embarks on a course of study. Also there may be business matters but they will proceed slowly and will need thinking about rather than rushing in boldly.

Reversed Meaning

This may indicate trouble to come for the Page of Cups (see upright description). There may be some studying which has to be done or an exam which must be passed. This is more of a chore than a pleasure.

KNIGHT OF CUPS

Knight of Cups

Meaning

A kindly, good natured youngish man, possibly fair haired. A Man who has feelings of love and affection for the Questioner is coming to or going away from the Questioner. The Questioner's lover or husband could have a journey ahead of him. Changes with regard to romance and relationships *may* soon be on the way.

Reversed Meaning

Love could be fading; a lover could be unfaithful, unloving or just not in a position at present to do what the Questioner wants.

Queen of Cups

Meaning

This woman will bring love and comfort to the Questioner. She is a good friend to the Questioner of either sex and will do her best to help in any situation. However, she may be somewhat possessive and materialistic. She should be maternal and home-loving and especially fond of animals. Either way up, she may be a bit spoiled and selfish.

Reversed Meaning

This lady may be disappointed in love in the near future, or intrinsically unable to give her affections freely. Possibly she is not sincere, she may be greedy, materialistic and jealous, it may be that she has been hurt before and is holding back rather than be hurt again.

KING OF CUPS

King of Cups

Meaning
Probably, but not necessarily, fair or reddish in hair and skin colouring.

Lover or husband, kindly warmhearted man who cares for the Questioner. Could be a bit possessive but would be successful and happy in love relationships himself and would make other people around him happy too. This man could be rather self indulgent and not always too reliable, although he is affectionate by nature.

Reversed Meaning
Probably quite caring and well meaning but not really that reliable. This could indicate to the Questioner that he is losing interest in this relationship or is not in a position to do much to help the Questioner. There could be jealousy or possessiveness here and the King could himself be a loser in the game of love.

4

THE SUIT OF STAVES

The suit of Staves (or Wands) is associated with negotiations of one kind or another. This may be to do with business, legal matters, clubs and societies, neighbourhood events or family business matters. Overseas travel is associated with some of the Stave cards, otherwise plenty of local trips and journeys are indicated. Creativity in the form of words is represented by these cards too. Often property dealings, home decorations and renovations are indicated by the appearance of Stave cards.

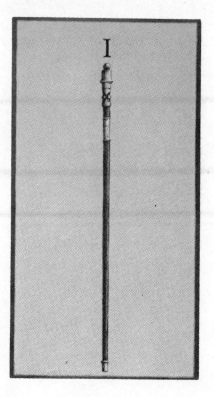

Ace of Staves

Meaning
This is the birth of an idea, even in some cases the birth of a child.
There could be a significant letter or phone call to do with business
– or businesslike matters. This should bring good news, and
should be the beginning of a successful enterprise.

Reversed Meaning
Indicates a new beginning but there will be problems attached. It is
still worth doing, but possibly the time is not quite right just now.

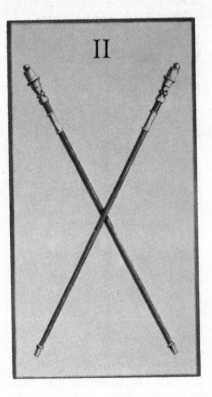

Two of Staves

Meaning
This could be a partnership or some sort of joint arrangement which will come into being but, in my experience, this has something to do with property or premises and may indicate a good property deal to come. Watch out for the competition though! There may also be a proud man who is, or shortly will be, important in the Questioner's life.

Reversed Meaning
Delays in the sale or purchase of property. Possibly a badly starred business partnership. Wait and try again another time. There may be unexpected news. A proud man may cause trouble.

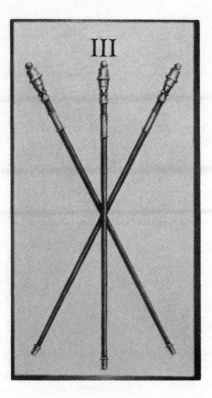

Three of Staves

Meaning
A new deal, new job or new beginning. There could be travel in
connection with work, or just an important letter or phone call
with good news on the way. Marriages and partnerships will go
well in future.

Reversed Meaning
Wait, try again later. There will be nothing good about going
ahead with business matters just now.

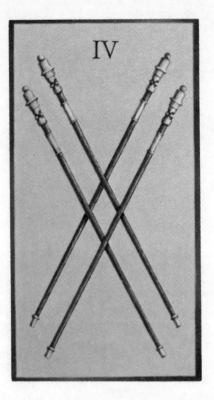

Four of Staves

Meaning
This is a card of security and of putting down roots. It may indicate
the purchase of a house or premises, or it may just indicate a good
holiday in the near future. There could be a house-warming soon.

Reversed Meaning
Similar to above but may be delayed or surrounded by problems.

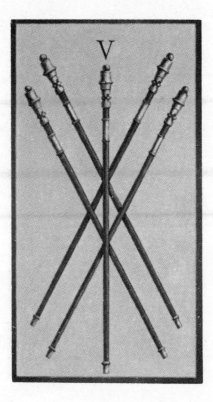

Five of Staves

Meaning
Something of a struggle in matters of negotiation, however, despite the aggravation there should be a good outcome in the end. Courage and endurance may be needed before the Questioner arrives where he wants to be. Travel plans may have to be put back.

Reversed Meaning
Leave it, try again another time. There may be legal problems ahead.

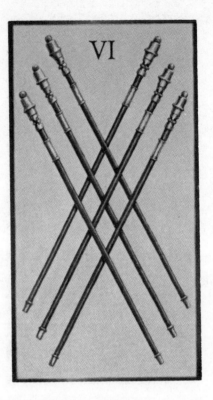

Six of Staves

Meaning
Victory! Great news! Legal battles will be won, negotiations will succeed, agreement will be reached and problems will be overcome.

Reversed Meaning
If there is a forthcoming battle, the other side will win. Leave it for the time being if you can, try again later. Other people may not do *their* jobs properly and that may affect your life in some way.

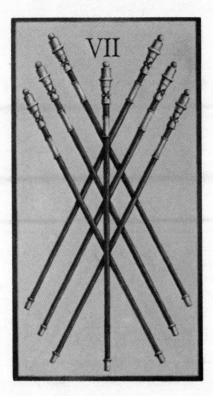

Seven of Staves

Meaning
Problems which can be overcome, but they may have to be isolated and sorted out one at a time. A constant battle, but with courage and determination this will be won. This may be a health problem or just the opposition of other people around the Questioner.

Reversed Meaning
There are just too many obstacles at the moment, try to sort out the worst of your problems now and leave chancy new decisions for another time. There could be some sort of puzzling or potentially embarrassing situation developing in the future.

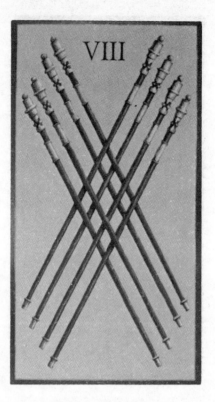

Eight of Staves

Meaning

There will soon be an expansion of the Questioner's horizons, taking the form of mind broadening experiences and new people. Travel is very likely and among the new faces and places there may well be friendship and love to be found.

Reversed Meaning

Cancelled plans. Do not move away from familiar ground just now. There could be jealousy and spite around the Questioner (or he may feel jealous himself soon). The Questioner may even be affected by strike action!

Nine of Staves

Meaning
The message to the Questioner from this card is to hang on to what
he or she has got. There will not be too much opportunity to
expand one's life and horizons just at the moment as one may be
surrounded by people who are making demands. The best bet is to
stay put, be prudent and keep the present lifestyle intact. This
card shows the Questioner to be in a *temporarily* secure position.

Reversed Meaning
There is a danger of loss of status or loss of position with this card.
There may be illness on the way now.

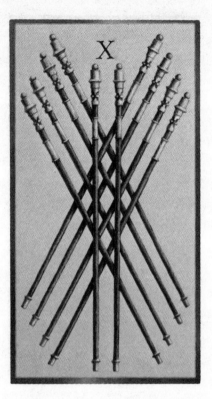

Ten of Staves

Meaning
There will be added burdens or more responsibility to come –
whichever way the Questioner likes to look at it. He or she could
receive a promotion to a more responsible position at work or
could find themselves lumbered in some way, though not
necessarily at work.

Reversed Meaning
Burdens can and will be put down shortly – but that promotion
and extra responsibility will not be forthcoming just yet.

Page of Staves

Meaning
An intelligent rather restless youngster who has charm and plenty to say. This card shows up when the Questioner is going on a journey. This will be fine if the Page is upright, but may involve a problem if the card is reversed. There may also be visitors (most probably young ones) from a long way off. There may also be surprising news on the way. Also letter and news about work and from old friends. Minor property or premises matters may go ahead now.

Reversed Meaning
There could be a problem for this youngster. There may be a delay or some sort of problem with regard to contracts or travel. Negotiations may be temporarily held up.

Knight of Staves

Meaning

Business or news to do with travel, also a visitor to or from afar. A move of house may be in the offing, changes are coming and they will require phone calls, letters and journeys. There may be romantic or business dealings with a chatty, pleasant young man.

Reversed Meaning

Something to do with travel or travellers may be disappointing. A promise may be broken. There may be a set-back with regard to property matters. A brown-haired young man may let the Questioner down or may prove to be insincere.

QUEEN OF STAVES

Queen of Staves

Meaning
A charming and clever woman, a good companion and a good talker. This lady is great fun, reliable in her affections and very loving but possibly a bit hard to pin down and possess as she has a definite mind of her own. She is a good business woman, adept in dealing with people and a reliable worker but not necessarily all that successful, she needs a good, helpful man behind her to boost her confidence in herself before she can really succeed.

Reversed Meaning
Either this lady is well meaning but unable to be reliable as a friend or successful in business because of circumstances, or she really is an unreliable and unfaithful type of person.

King of Staves

Meaning
Probably light to medium colouring, fair skinned with lightish hair, slimly built. An amusing, chatty, friendly man who is fond of the Questioner but not necessarily going to become heavily involved emotionally. This man is good company, will cheer the Questioner up and may be very helpful in the working environment. Good at selling, communicating or marketing.

Reversed Meaning
At worst this may be a sly liar, at best this man is unreliable and untrustworthy. He may be great fun but do not take him too seriously or get heavily involved with him in ways that matter. He may be full of promises but not willing (or able) to deliver the goods just now.

5

THE SUIT OF SWORDS

The Sword cards indicate trouble and strife, swift action to be taken, and health matters. Sometimes they represent travel over, or to, watery places. These cards can also indicate courage and authority figures as well as sadness and betrayal. The Swords get right to the heart of any matter, and for that reason they represent areas of life and experience which have to be taken very seriously.

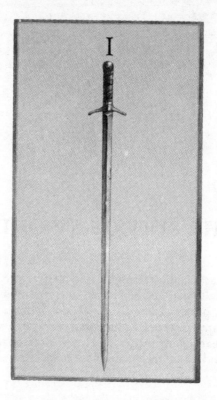

Ace of Swords

Meaning

This may indicate an operation, as the presence of this card can mean a cut to the body, or at least an injection. Like all Aces, this card may indicate the beginning of a new cycle but in this case it will be something all absorbing such as a very difficult but rewarding job, or a really passionate love affair. Whatever is coming to the Questioner, it will do so with quite a bang. There may also be power and justice coming to (or for) the Questioner.

Reversed Meaning

Similar to above, but the events which are on the way are likely to be milder and not so all absorbing. This could be a warning card that a business deal will turn out to be an absolute disaster. This can also show that the Questioner may take too much action in some way and may 'go over the top' so to speak, or react too strongly to a situation.

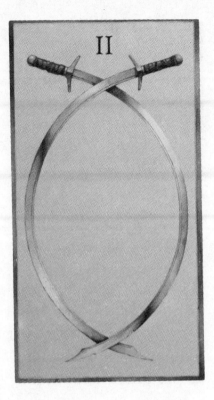

Two of Swords

Meaning
There is a strange situation going on when this card appears. The
Questioner cannot make a move and cannot see his way forward.
It is a card of suspension, no change, possibly of delay. If the
Questioner has fears about a relationship breaking up, or the loss
of a job, then the appearance of this card would give reassurance
that things would remain as they are. However, on the other hand
no improvement in life can be expected either at this time. There
may be an agreement, settlement or some sort of peace treaty.

Reversed Meaning
The end of stalemate, things are about to start moving. There may
be relief and release from a difficult situation now, or the
Questioner, or someone close, may travel away soon.

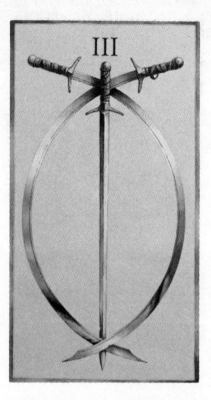

Three of Swords

Meaning

There may be loss or heartache to be faced. This could be the end of a relationship or some other sad event. Some say that this card indicates blood, therefore there could be illness or an operation coming soon.

Reversed Meaning

The end of a period of heartbreak, the beginning of learning to cope with a loss or rejection. There may be a minor surgical procedure soon. The Questioner may attend a funeral in the near future.

Four of Swords

Meaning
This is a card of recovery from illness. (It is amazing how often this card will come up near someone who is in hospital and it is always good news for the sick person.) The other indication is that the Questioner needs to take a break from present stressful situations.

Reversed Meaning
This is not too optimistic for a sick person as it indicates that the illness is still there and more treatment is needed. In other circumstances there may be recovery from financial losses.

Five of Swords

Meaning
This card shows quarrels, possibly even violence. There may be ruined plans and a rather bad time all round. Someone the Questioner loves may suddenly go away – possibly even overseas. There might be people who are jealous and spiteful to the Questioner.

Reversed Meaning
Similar to upright but the problem is probably passing from the Questioner's life shortly. The Questioner may attend a funeral shortly.

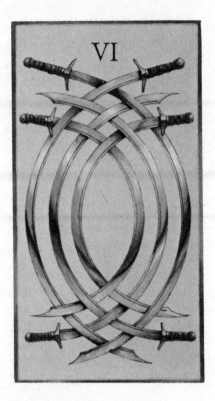

Six of Swords

Meaning
Travel over water, there could be an element of gradual release
from poverty or unhappiness now and a move or journey may be
the turning point. There may be a visitor from overseas coming
into the Questioner's life – check other cards nearby for this.

Reversed Meaning
Journeys – even holidays will be delayed. There may be financial
losses due to carelessness.

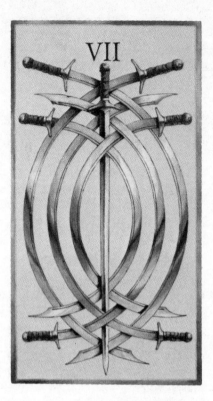

Seven of Swords

Meaning

This card is hard to interpret. It may indicate a robbery or rip-off to come or it may mean that the Questioner is due to gather up his resources, cut his losses and sort out some difficult situation once and for all. There is often legal or business advice here – but there is also the desire to escape from overwhelming problems.

Reversed Meaning

There will be advice (possibly legal) forthcoming soon. However, beware of thieves.

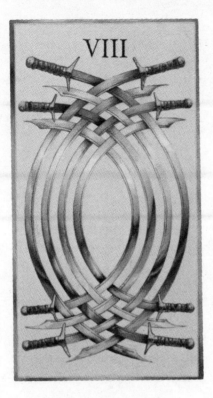

Eight of Swords

Meaning
The Questioner is temporarily tied down and cannot do much to change the circumstances. This could be due to all sorts of reasons and the only thing to do is to wait and see how things go for a while before attempting to make major changes. There should be light at the end of the tunnel here.

Reversed Meaning
Restrictions will soon lift but depressions and hard times must be coped with first. There may be accidents, disappointments or even deaths in the Questioner's environment.

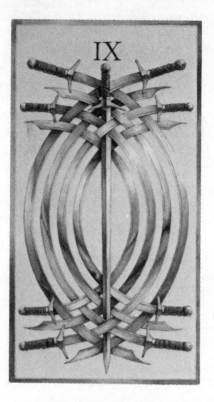

Nine of Swords

Meaning
There could be illness, even a miscarriage or some nagging worry.
I find that this card often shows up shortly before the Questioner's
mother gets into difficulties or causes problems for others.

Reversed Meaning
The worry and sleepless nights will shortly come to an end. There
may be unpleasant rumours being put around about the Questioner.

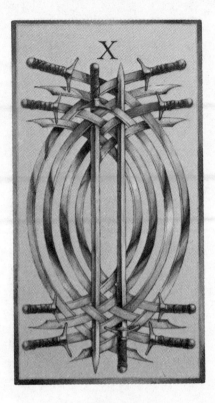

Ten of Swords

Meaning
There will be treachery – a stab in the back. This is an unfortunate card as it can indicate divorce, work problems and general unhappiness. There could be a forced change coming, not of the Questioner's choosing.

Reversed Meaning
Minor disappointment, a person may try to slander the Questioner or may let him or her down. However, hard times will come to an end soon and in the case of ill health, there will soon be recovery.

PAGE OF SWORDS

Page of Swords

Meaning
This is an active, possibly sporty child, who is dark haired. There may be good news about business but the Questioner is being told to keep his eyes open because either opportunity, or possibly scandal, are on the way. A contract may shortly need to be signed.

Reversed Meaning
The young person described in the upright section may have problems to face. Indicates arguments and problems but these could be settled soon. There could be disappointments regarding work and business matters, especially those concerning contracts. There may be someone unpleasant who is spying on the Questioner and hoping to land the Questioner in trouble.

KNIGHT OF SWORDS

Knight of Swords

Meaning

A tough, brave and very intelligent young man may help the Questioner soon. There will be a young and energetic environment. Possibly swift changes and decisions to be made soon. An assertive dark young man may come along soon. The Questioner may make hasty decisions or sudden changes in the near future.

Reversed Meaning

This could indicate an aggressive, destructive, argumentative young man, or just an active and ambitious man who has temporary difficulties. Arguments coming soon and swift action to be taken shortly. There could be some medical or surgical treatment soon.

QUEEN OF SWORDS

Queen of Swords

Meaning
A sharp, clever woman, either a teacher, doctor or lawyer. She should be good to the Questioner but although helpful with the kind of problem which requires professional help, she might be a bit too cool and prickly to make a good loving companion. It depends really on the Questioner's priorities at the time of the reading. This lady commands respect.

Reversed Meaning
This lady is sharp and unpleasant. She may be professionally in opposition to the Questioner, or just a strong and difficult influence in the Questioner's life. She may be cold-hearted and possibly spiteful.

KING OF SWORDS

King of Swords

Meaning
Possibly dark haired and rather sharp featured, this could well be a doctor, lawyer or professional man who is about to have some important influence on the Questioner's life. Of course, he may be the Questioner's boss – however, any of the Kings would fit into that category. This man could bring problems which have to be dealt with, literally speaking, there could be trouble ahead which he may (or may not) help the Questioner to deal with. He appears to lack a sense of humour and to be a tough, uncompromising professional man; however, there could be a good reason to need a man like this on one's side in the near future. Put it this way; if I was faced with some sort of financial or medical problem, I would be quite glad to see this card turn up in a spread as it would show me that I would soon find the right man for the job in hand.

Reversed Meaning

This is an aggressive man who is bent on stirring up trouble – he may be the lawyer who is representing the opposition in an impending law suit. He may be a particularly unhelpful medical or professional man whom the Questioner will shortly be up against, or he may be closely involved in the Questioner's private or business life. He may not actually be all that evil, just angry because he cannot help much at present. If this is so, then the Questioner may expect aggression, tantrums, possibly even violence from this man.

6

THE SUIT OF COINS

The Suit of Coins is associated with money, goods and services, the organization of work and of business; also matters relating to the Questioner's status and his or her larger possessions such as property.

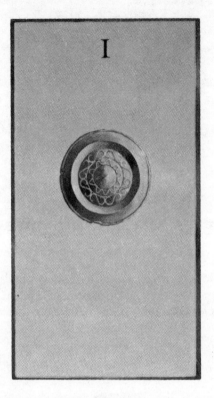

Ace of Coins

Meaning
Money coming to the Questioner, this may be a win, bonus or a raise or it may be associated with a better job – a step up in the Questioner's financial position. It could be a letter about money but the news will be good.

Reversed Meaning
Same as upright but the significance (and amounts of cash) will be less.

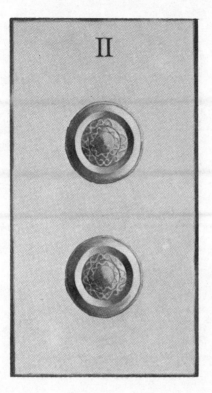

Two of Coins

Meaning

Separation, possibly the breakup of a partnership or of a home. Property may be divided either by agreement or by law. Alternatively, this card may indicate a lack of ability either through the Questioner's nature, or circumstances, to cope with all the different demands that are being made on him or her. The Questioner will be borrowing from Peter to pay Paul.

Reversed Meaning

In my experience this card is much the same either way up, except that the problem may be coming to an end if the card is reversed.

Three of Coins

Meaning
Buying a home, or extending or improving of property or premises. Also success in business due to cashing in on some talent or learned skill.

Reversed Meaning
Same as above but beset by problems, probably indicating that the Questioner has bitten off more than he can chew.

Four of Coins

Meaning
Financial security is on the way, but there may be too much emphasis on money in the Questioner's outlook on life at this time. This card also shows that the *long term* financial outlook is going to be good.

Reversed Meaning
Money may be short, security will be hard to come by in the short term. Exam failures and delays in payments are possible.

Five of Coins

Meaning
A sense of loss and loneliness prevails, however there is warmth
and love to be found but probably not from the place where the
Questioner most wishes it to come. Oddly enough, affairs and
romances flourish when this card shows up but they are not going
to be deeply satisfying emotionally. Financial loss is the most
likely outcome from this card.

Reversed Meaning
A period of loss and loneliness will end soon.

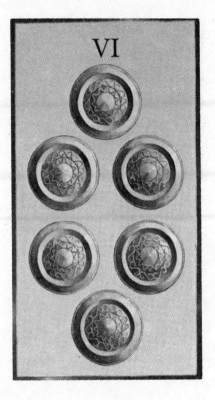

Six of Coins

Meaning

This indicates that money will have to be shared out soon. Other cards nearby will help to indicate why, but it may be the result of a divorce, redundancy or an inheritance. The Questioner's finances will have to be sorted out, there may be too many people around who are trying to drain the Questioner of money or of energy. There is another meaning to this card and that is of benevolence, i.e. that the Questioner will be in such a good position that he will be able and willing to help out other people. Personally, I have found that the former is more likely to be the case.

Reversed Meaning

Similar to upright but the problem may be passing away by now.

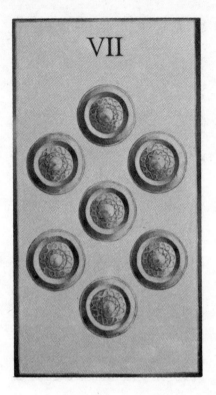

Seven of Coins

Meaning
This card indicates slow growth, achievement or advancement by dint of long term efforts. Therefore, hard work will bring just rewards – keep at it. Even if things are bad now, don't give up, keep trying.

Reversed Meaning
A period of hard work will come to an end soon, frankly it is just not worth battling on just now. Wait and try again later.

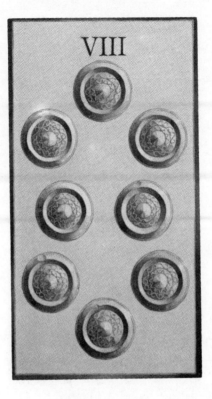

Eight of Coins

Meaning
A new job or promotion, there may be a raise or just praise. The Questioner will soon learn a new skill which will be relevant to a future career.

Reversed Meaning
Problem at work, could just be that the Questioner's present job will come to an end soon or will need to take a new direction. The Questioner may be put into a position where he has to learn new methods whether he wants to or not.

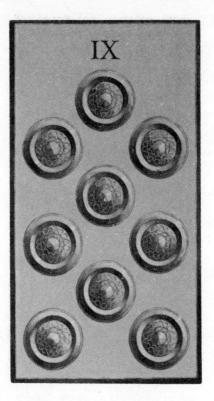

Nine of Coins

Meaning
Money and success are on the way. This will be a good time to buy goods for the home. Domestic matters will go well.

Reversed Meaning
There will be no success and not much money coming from this project. The Questioner may be selling some of his belongings soon.

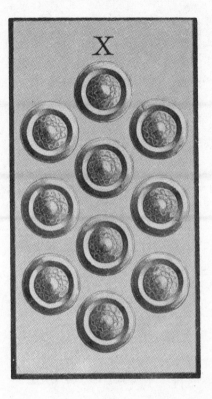

Ten of Coins

Meaning
This card brings money and success but also great pleasure from
personal achievement. Can bring travel in connection with
business and it can also indicate a good future marriage and family
life. Commercial matters will be an integral part of any marriage
when this card is involved.

Reversed Meaning
Some success is on the way. There may be a gift coming or some
sort of charitable benefit such as winning a raffle prize. There may
even be a state (or private) pension on the way.

PAGE OF COINS

Page of Coins

Meaning
A steady business-like youngster probably with very dark hair.

This card brings news about money matters and possibly travel; however, in this case it would be on business rather than for pleasure. There may be news of a promotion at work too. A youngster could have some good news soon, or may do something to make people proud of him.

Reversed Meaning
The young person described above could have some problems to come. There could be some slight temporary shortage of money, also business and money news will be poor for a while.

KNIGHT OF COINS

Knight of Coins

Meaning
This should be a youngish man with a cautious nature. A young man coming with news about business, money, etc. Even travel and business are possible now due to the restless nature of the Knight card.

Reversed Meaning
Problems with regard to work, money or people who have great ideas that cost the Questioner money. Could be a warning not to travel on business just now.

QUEEN OF COINS

Queen of Coins

Meaning
This lady is money-minded. She may be comfortably off, or just
determined to be so. She commands respect because of her status
and possessions – or would like to do so. She is a skilled negotiator
and an honest and reliable business woman. She would be a
comfortable and warm-hearted love companion, but only to the
man who will give her a decent standard of living.

Reversed Meaning
This lady will win if involved in a fight against the Questioner,
especially if money is involved. She is tough and materialistic.
However, she may be perfectly kind and reasonable, but
temporarily down on her own luck.

KING OF COINS

King of Coins

Meaning
Dark haired and complexioned, possibly a rather thick-set build.
A sound solid citizen, conservative and reliable if rather boring.
He should have good business sense but will be cautious rather
than a gambler or experimenter. He should be very close to his
family. He is basically kindly but may be somewhat mean, over-
careful, or nervous of spending unnecessarily. He is a tough but
honest bargainer and negotiator.

Reversed Meaning
A hard headed business man who is not on the Questioner's side.
Alternatively, he may look steady but actually turn out to be a
loser. He could be mean, untrustworthy, unfair or possessive. He
may even be quite a good person who is temporarily down on his
luck.

7

QUICK CLUES TO THE MINOR ARCANA

The Numbered Cards

Cups: Love and possessions
Staves: Words and negotiations
Swords: Action and problems
Coins: Money and status

* * *

Aces Beginnings, birth of something new.

2s Partnerships and relationships, starting and ending.

3s Beginning and ending of enterprises; home, business, relationships – often with teamwork involved as opposed to alone.

4s Stability; making a situation secure, putting down roots. The Four of Cups is the exception here as it indicates dissatisfaction.

5s Loss, sadness, regret, looking back to what has been. Giving up something, changing personal attitudes in line with circumstances.

6s Moves forward; either by travelling (Swords),

finalizing outstanding financial settlements (Coins), family matters (Cups), or gathering up one's courage for future challenges (Staves).

7s Move forward cautiously and sort out real values from childish desires. Work and be patient, take advice, take care.

8s Expansion of present world. Changes in job, home environment or personal attitude may be necessary. A *gradual* move away from old unhappiness and failures.

9s Satisfaction and security; hanging on to what one has got. Perhaps hanging on a bit too long or finding out that what one has worked and schemed to achieve is not all that wonderful after all (if the cards are reversed).

10s Complete happiness, achievement, love, success, money and satisfaction. Gaining the full benefit out of the joy of living, gaining one's heart's desire – or losing the lot!

The Court Cards

Cups: Love, marriage, possessions and home life, also long term education.
Staves: Negotiations, travel, communications.
Swords: Activity, aggression, achievement and trouble.
Coins: Money, possessions, business, building for the long term future.

* * *

King of Cups Fair man, loving/uncaring.

King of Staves Medium colouring, fluent talker, reliable/unreliable.

King of Swords Dark man, active, clever, helpful/nasty.

King of Coins Dark man, good in business, generous/mean.

Queen of Cups Fair woman, kind, loving/refuses to care.

Queen of Staves Medium colouring, friendly, talkative/gossipy.

Queen of Swords Dark woman, clever, helpful/unpleasant.

Queen of Coins Dark woman, good with money/mean.

Knight of Cups Love coming/going.

Knight of Staves Move of house, travel or visitors.

Knight of Swords Swift changes, unexpected and sudden help, fighting, violence.

Knight of Coins Money and business matters, maybe somebody to help with this soon.

Page of Cups Fair loving/unloving child, a course of study or contemplation.

Page of Staves Medium coloured child, travel, news, perhaps a business 'representative'.

Page of Swords Dark active child, sharp words, swift action. Verbal or written good/bad news.

Page of Coins Dark placid child, money matters, news of money/family or other long-standing and important interests.

8

THE MAJOR ARCANA

The Major Arcana is so powerful in its imagery that it can be used on its own, without the Minor Arcana, even though there are only twenty-two cards. Many Readers will give a Major Arcana reading followed by another reading using the whole pack. This gives them the outline of the Questioner's problems and lifestyle before going on to give the complete reading. In a mixture of Major and Minor cards, it is interesting to note how many of the Major cards appear and where.

Even though packs vary somewhat, the overall symbolism of the Major cards remains the same (i.e. the Emperor may be dressed or seated differently in different packs, but he is still the Emperor!).

There is a certain amount of controversy these days about whether to give reverse readings for cards and I believe that the majority of professional Readers *do not* reverse their cards at all. The idea is that all the cards have their good and bad (weak or strong might be a better description) aspects, and this is especially true of the Major Arcana cards. I have broken the explanations down into 'positive' and 'negative' to make them a bit easier for the novice reader to understand and the 'negative' can be given as a reversed reading if so desired. Frankly, I feel that each card encompasses both sides within its nature, but I leave it to you to experiment with these cards for yourself.

O
THE FOOL

Positive

This can be shown as the first or last card in the Major Arcana. I
tend to think of it as the first card as it represents a fresh start or the
discovery of talents and abilities that the Questioner did not know
were there. It represents a person stepping out into a new future
which could take them anywhere. It is a chance to start again and it
can be applied to any aspect of life, such as a new relationship, a
new area to live in, a new job, a change of direction generally. Its
message is that a new door is opening and there will be challenges
ahead which can be taken advantage of. The Fool can also tell of
fun ahead and light hearted enjoyable people and events to come.
However, even as a 'positive' card, there is a warning not to be
rash, or to rush in to a new situation in a blind and undisciplined

manner. Positive or negative, the Fool tells the Questioner that he is going to have to use his willpower and to exercise restraint in some future situation.

Negative

There is a clear warning here to give thought and consideration to any new situation. The Questioner will be tempted to act in an immature, possibly even irrational, manner, and may become obsessed by some craze which leads them into extravagance and loss. There may be an overwhelming passion for somebody tremendously exciting, but there will be problems attached to this affair which *must* be taken into consideration before plunging in. If the warnings are ignored then at best, the outcome will make the Questioner look and feel like a prize idiot, and at worst this could be tragic.

I
THE MAGICIAN

Positive

This card depicts new opportunities, it may be the start of an enterprise or even of an important relationship, though in general, I feel that it has more to do with business matters and worldly affairs than with love and romance. There may be several courses of action to be looked at in the near future, and thought must be paid to new decisions and actions. There will soon be a chance to use skills and education in a practical manner, but there should be some kind of politics or salesmanship involved in this somewhere.

A friend once described the Magician as indicating 'a bold step' and this is probably right as there is a somewhat chancy element attached to this card. It tells the Questioner to go ahead and blind them all with science, use the new found confidence and have a go. All in all, an important new cycle in the Questioner's life, especially that part of it which is carried on outside the home. There is definitely a feeling of the Questioner being urged to put ideas into practice because there will be great rewards for use of one's imagination, original ideas, flair, art, craft or subtlety that he or she possesses. This card could show up just as the Questioner is goint to start a business using the skills and talents they possess. This is a good example because it pre-supposes self-reliance, flexibility and the ability to choose one's own action. It also shows determination to see the task through to the end.

THE MAGICIAN

Negative
The warning here is not to miss an opportunity that is coming up.
Also to look carefully at any new enterprise which is presented to
the Questioner by *other people*. They may not be all that honest.
There is always an air of trickery around the Magician, either the
good trickery of the successful salesman or the heartlessness of the
'cowboy' or 'con artist'. If this card depicts a person around the
Questioner, he may be about to take on just the right one for the
job; alternatively, the Questioner may go headlong into a business
where he may find himself being controlled by a team of crooks or
fools! The warning as with all the cards is that everything in life can
go either way. Although consideration is essential before action
when this card shows up, especially if it is upright and in a
prominent part of a spread, then for goodness sake have a go!

II
THE HIGH PRIESTESS

Positive

If students of the occult finds this card upright and in a prominent place in the reading, then they are being told to go ahead with their studies; that they *have* the ability and will make positive and helpful use of it. The Priestess has both intuition and common-sense, there is a feeling of ancient knowledge about her, about the hidden and mysterious things in life. I feel that if this card shows up when decisions are to be made, then one should follow one's feelings and let one's natural intuition be the guide, also to make allowances for somebody else's intuition particularly if they are close and trusted friends.

The Priestess also indicates scholarship in its widest sense. The card can fortell a period of study to come and of a good teacher who will be very helpful to the Questioner. It may point to a particular person about to help the Questioner, this would be a woman who is clever, rather remote but informative, if not very motherly in manner, a professionally qualified person most likely. The Questioner may take on some of the mantle of the High Priestess and find himself in a position to apply common sense and understanding. The card is also associated with integrity and honesty, so although the tongue may be sharp, the sentiments and the heart are in the right place. Of course, the Priestess, like all the cards, is somewhat androgynous, which means that 'she' may actually be a 'he'!

There is one other rather tantalizing point about the Priestess which is that it points out to the Questioner that they are not yet in possession of all the facts. The Reader must note the area of the spread in which this card falls and tell the Questioner that something pertaining to this subject has yet to be revealed.

Negative
The negative side is the opposite of cool commonsensical control, i.e. uncontrolled emotional outbursts and stupid careless remarks. Selfishness and impatience make for rows, and the Questioner is reminded to make sure that they really know what they are talking about before getting into an argument. There is a feeling of high sexual tension here as the image of the High Priestess is of an untouchable and apparently cool natured woman which makes us wonder what passions may be boiling away under her habit! However, even if uncontrolled passion is about to enter one's life, there could be something to learn, even if it is only to improve one's sexual technique!

Another negative aspect of this card sometimes shows up when a female Questioner is being so mindful of her family's needs that she neglects her own. She is being told not to sacrifice so much time and money on them, especially on their education, as they would learn some good practical lessons from life if she left them alone and attended to *her own* requirements a bit more.

III
THE EMPRESS

Positive
This card represents feminity in abundance, like the goddess Venus, with all her sexual charms on the one hand, and a plump

loving mother caring for her children on the other. On a more
down-to-earth note, there could be a child on the way when this
card shows up. If the Questioner is too old to have children, this
can indicate the birth of a grandchild, nephew or niece. In a man's
reading, the Empress represents a warm and loving woman who
makes him feel that all's right with the world. If the Questioner is
thinking of getting married, then the Empress will show that the
marriage will take place and be satisfying and happy. If there is
nothing dramatic going on in the Questioner's love life, then this
card shows that there is material satisfaction and comfort around
the corner.

As a situation rather than an actual woman, the theme of
fertility and abundance still counts. Like the planet Venus in
astrology, the Empress is concerned with fruits of the earth,
personal values and possessions, especially large and important
ones. Therefore, this could show up when the Questioner is just

about to move from town to country, or to buy a house with a garden. If this is the case, then the move would be beneficial. There could be more money after a pretty lean period, or just a feeling of satisfaction with oneself and one's life. A generous warm and satisfying card which is especially concerned with ownership of goods, that is of material things rather than spiritual or mental activity. The 'proprietary' feelings attached to the Empress extend to people in the sense that one says 'This is *my* child', or 'Let me introduce you to *my* wife'!

Negative

There is not much that is negative about this card but it can suggest that one is overdoing the self-indulgence bit and will regret this later. It also tends to indicate possessiveness and jealousy born of fear of rejection and loss. There is also a strong possibility of either infertility (probably temporary) or on the other hand an unwanted pregnancy. I often find that sterilization, vasectomy and abortion, or operations involving the reproductive organs, show up when this card is reversed in an important position in a spread. This does not indicate whether these situations are chosen by or forced upon the Questioner, just the fact that they are there. There can be emotional disappointments, disenchantment with a new property, especially if it has no garden – the Empress *likes* growing things. There could be financial loss, therefore no abundance and short shrift for a time.

IIII
THE EMPEROR

Positive

The Emperor is definitely the boss! If this card represents a person who is a part of or is about to enter the Questioner's sphere of interest, then the Questioner will definitely not be able to ignore him. This man might be a skilled business man, an elder statesman in government, or a powerful, firm but benevolent husband or father figure. If a woman is enquiring about a man she has just met and the Emperor card shows up, she can be sure that he *is* all he appears to be and will stand by her and support her. He is strong and steady by nature, with both the will and the ability to take charge in any situation. He is a good manager and reliable partner. He may not be too much fun at times, and will probably not be very talkative and entertaining, but he will stand fast and cope with any situation. Think of Jack Hawkins as the captain in 'The

Cruel Sea' and you will be on the right track!

As a situation rather than a person, the Emperor represents the ability to influence people and events. The Questioner may take on some of the Emperor's personality and find him or herself moving steadily up into a position of power and influence. This indicates a firm base, a sound financial position and perhaps a secure and respected position in the community. The Questioner will be able to reach his goals and will use intelligence and reason, rather than make emotional or even intuitive judgements.

Negative
There is not much that *is* negative about this card. However, if the Questioner wants to know whether a particular person is as reliable and responsible as he seems to be, and the card comes out reversed, then I would suggest that he is not, at least for the

moment, all that he is cracked up to be. This may be because he is not as strong a character as he wants others to think he is, not as reliable as the Questioner would like him to be; or is just temporarily out of stock of stiff upper lips. The reverse of the Emperor is immaturity and a lack of concentration, the inability to finish what has been started, too much dependence upon others instead of self reliance and faith in one's own abilities. This man's apparent weakness may be due to poor health which could, of course, be a temporary situation or a sad warning that a strong and good man is not going to be able to continue with a full and active life.

V
THE HIEROPHANT

Positive

The ideas behind this card are rather difficult to put across, as the general feeling is of kindness, conformity and spiritual guidance. The Hierophant *may* turn up as a person in the Questioner's life, but this would be unusual, somehow he seems to represent situations rather than people. However, if he does, then he may literally be a teacher (especially in the sense that a Rabbi is a teacher) or even a personnel officer. He will advise the Questioner to take a good look at his motives and even to pray for guidance. When the guidance does come, it will emphasize right from wrong and will be along the lines of conventional, possibly religious, thought.

As a situation, the Hierophant represents conventional behaviour. Therefore if a Questioner wants to know whether the person he or she fancies wants a conventional marriage, or prefers to live together and still go out with others, then the Hierophant, upright and in a relevant part of the spread, will definitely show that the conventional is wanted. If there is some doubt in the Questioner's mind about how to go about achieving his aims in life, the Hierophant will show that the traditional ways will lead to success. In fact, tradition, spirituality and following the dictates of God, one's conscience and the tried and tested methods of working and living are going to be the most successful in this case. There will be kindness and help from people around the Questioner. The older, more staid people will be the ones to offer useful advice and help. If this card shows up when the Questioner's affairs are being held up, it signifies that the delay will not be for much longer.

Negative

There really is not much that is negative about this card except to say that the Questioner may be his own worst enemy by being too timid and too aware of other people's requirements while neglecting his own. It is strange that the two cards who represent people who train and teach us (the Hierophant and the High Priestess) should also warn against being *too* kind-hearted. They are telling us that making excuses for other people's weaknesses is not going to do anyone any good and a dose of firmness may be of more benefit in the long run to all concerned. It is better to stand up for yourself when you know you are right. The other problems are of hypocrisy and self doubt. Be honest, at least with yourself, *that* is the message here.

When the Hierophant is reversed, then non-conformity will be the order of the day. For instance, if the Questioner wants to know

whether the person they are interested in desires marriage, then
the answer will be negative. There is also the feeling that a more
relaxed attitude to matters of business may be more productive,
therefore, the Questioner would be better not to put things on a
firm traditional footing, but just let things slide along for a while
and see what turns up. In other words, do not try to coerce
someone into marriage. or into strict modes of operating which
will not suit. The Questioner should be prepared to accept novel
ways of thinking and not be captive to their own ideas or too full of
their own opinions.

VI
THE LOVERS

Positive
There are two distinct and very different messages from this card.
On the one hand it can mean exactly what it looks like, i.e. that
love, romance and passion are coming to the Questioner. In this
context it means that a relationship is just around the corner or one
which is worrying the Questioner will bloom into love and
marriage. On a milder note this card means friendship and
harmony. Therefore, if it shows up in an area relating to work, it
would mean that relationships with colleagues at work or with
business partners will be happy and productive. As well as
meaning attraction, this card is often interpreted as beauty. When
one finds someone attractive, they become beautiful even if they
are, strictly speaking, not good looking. If there has been a parting,
for whatever reason, the Lovers card indicates that the partners
will soon be reunited.

The other meaning attached to the Lovers is of *choice*. This
means that the Questioner is soon going to have to choose
between two people, two courses of action, two jobs or two of
anything, and that the matter of choosing is going to be very
important in its outcome. The obvious impression is of choosing
between sacred and profane love, and this may well be the case;
but the general idea is that the choice has some sort of right or
wrong influence, selfish or unselfish, easy or tough. A common
matter of choice for women these days is whether to have a career,
or opt for an old fashioned family life.

Negative
When the Lover appears reversed, it can mean a temporary or
permanent parting, the end of a relationship rather than the

beginning, but this will be made clearer by reference to the rest of the reading. It also warns of making a mistake, tying oneself up with the wrong person or for the wrong reasons. The Questioner will remain frustrated in their desires (carnal or otherwise) if they do not make an effort or make their feelings a bit more obvious to the other person. Another problem is infatuation, wanting someone who is clearly wrong for all concerned.

VII
THE CHARIOT

Positive

The Chariot is associated with a time of hard work and major effort, and it is often retro-active, which means that it is just as likely to show the phase which has recently passed by as to indicate something which has yet to come. Either way, it is associated with

a struggle, and a time when one does not know whether one is on one's head or one's heels. There could be a great ordeal here, a time of strain and overwork but the feeling is that the outcome makes all the effort worthwhile. This may be a course of action which is deliberately chosen by the Questioner like going into business or moving house, thereby incurring a lot of work in getting the project off the ground. The troubles may, of course, be something not of the Questioner's choosing, which would mean dealing with a knotty problem which is definitely going to need hard work, patience and endurance to solve. The feeling is that a victory is achieved here despite setbacks. In a way it is quite a simple card to interpret, because it means that things have been, still are, or about to be, very hard to handle for a while – but that the outcome is good. The general feeling of the Chariot is of purposeful activity.

On a more practical note, this card often shows up when the Questioner is about to buy a new vehicle, or to have one MoT'd or set to rights, in this case it is a good omen. The Chariot may also indicate that the Questioner will be travelling soon, possibly in connection with work. I have noticed that vehicles – planes, boats, even bicycles – enter the life of the Questioner after this card turns up in a spread.

Negative

The meaning here is much the same as above, but the Questioner has less chance of winning outright, or the struggle is going against them at the moment. This does not mean that it will always be that way, things may change. The one sure thing about the Chariot is that it shows a time of tension and hard work which cannot and will not go on forever. If this card *is* reversed, then the problems are more likely to have been presented *to*, rather than chosen *by*, the Questioner. This card sometimes predicts problems with regard to vehicles.

VIII
JUSTICE

Positive

The meaning of this card is actually quite obvious – it represents justice, fairness, balance, etc. This card often comes up when there are legal matters to be dealt with, and on the whole it can be taken to mean that the outcome will be good. If the card shows up *reversed* in the ninth position in an Astrological spread (see page 147), it would not be good news legally.

The Justice card does not restrict itself strictly to legal matters, it encompasses all matters relating to fairness and justice in the wider sense. For instance, this would be a terrific card to have if a partnership or joint venture is about to be entered. Although it is stretching things somewhat, even a forthcoming marriage could show up with this card, as it would show that the union would bring harmony and a feeling of completeness and balance to the couple involved. If the Questioner is involved in any kind of argument, or has been in any way accused of doing something wrong, he will soon be proved right. There could be agreements through discussion, or a situation where the Questioner acts in an honest manner when others around them do not and this honesty, loyalty and idealism are shown to be right.

Negative

This is one of those cards which does need some extra
consideration if it comes out reversed, as it does appear to reverse
the meaning of the upright version. That is to say, legal problems
will continue or will not be resolved to the Questioner's
satisfaction. If there are no legal matters concerning the Questioner,
then he or she is being warned of some sort of unfair treatment or
unfair accusation to come. There could be a lack of promotion, or
some other setback due to somebody who is engaging in
underhand politics. The Questioner may have to apologise to
someone or make a special effort to keep the peace.

VIIII
THE HERMIT

Positive

This is not an easy card to interpret as its meaning is subtle, it also tends to give advice to the Questioner rather than show a forthcoming event. It indicates that the Questioner will need to take some time out to think things over.

There could be an important decision to make, or just one of those times when there will be a need for reflection and consideration of long term aims and ambitions. This may show that the Questioner would benefit from the advice of an expert, or just a sensible and sympathetic friend. He or she could do well to withdraw from active life for a while in order to meditate, pray and give some thought to the larger issues of life and death. There is another meaning to this card and that means that the Questioner will need to be cautious and prudent in some forthcoming situation. This card contains an element of self denial, and it all fits in with the idea of living quietly for a while, possibly doing without something or someone. It can mean a time of loneliness

ahead, which may be self-imposed. There could even be a time of convalescence. The retreat from life and company may be self-imposed or imposed from outside, but it will be beneficial if the Questioner makes the most of the peaceful and reflective period.

Negative

In my experience there are two or three meanings to this. Firstly, there may be a petulant refusal of help in a difficult situation. The Questioner could turn away from family or friends, and cut his nose off to spite his face.

Secondly, there could be a failure to grow up and see things as they really are. Both of these are the kind of state of mind which results from a person being hurt or rejected in some way, jealousy or fear are likely to be at the back of this behaviour.

The third idea is that the Questioner might be left alone, bereaved or let down by a lover or partner and may feel very lonely, rejected and down-hearted for a while. Sometimes the question, 'Is he coming back?' is answered by a reversed Hermit (plus other pointers) as being 'no'.

X
WHEEL OF FORTUNE

Positive

Whenever the Wheel of Fortune appears in a spread it signifies change. The Questioner is being told that nothing stays the same forever, and in this particular case changes are definitely on the way. It would be nice to suggest that the changes are for the better, but this is not necessarily so. Just think of a ferris wheel in a fairground, the little seats with their cargo of laughing passengers are travelling *up* on one side of the wheel, at the same time others are travelling *down* the other side. Therefore let us be optimists and suggest that the Wheel indicates a turn for the better, a chance coming from out of the blue, a stroke of luck, great opportunity or even a godsend. Certainly this card shows that events related to the sphere of life it represents in the spread are going to be changing.

Most Readers like to see this as an optimistic card, but it may not be so – the best that one can say is that any sudden setbacks can be viewed as a challenge which give the Questioner a chance to grow in whatever area of life is affected by the changes to come. The *placement* of this card in a spread is actually more important than the card itself as it is meant to show *where* the greatest changes will come.

Negative
There really isn't a reverse meaning for this card except that if the
upright Wheel can be taken to represent an upturn in fortunes,
then the reversed Wheel may bring unexpected setbacks. This
may herald the end of a rather easy phase and the beginning of a
stressful time to come. There are challenges here and the
Questioner will be given the chance to rise to the occasion or let
himself become downhearted.

XI
STRENGTH

Positive
On a very simple and straightforward level this card shows that
somebody who has been ill is going to recover soon. If the person
indicated in the spread has been feeling tired, down-hearted or has

just not been coping with things too well lately, then things are bound to improve.

On another level, this card shows that the Questioner will be able to overcome future obstacles, have the courage and resolution to cope. There will be calm perseverence and determination, especially when under pressure. Plans may be put into action soon, achievements and success lie ahead. This good card to have when interviews and exams are due.

Above all, the mood of the Strength card is of quiet courage of the unspectacular kind in the face of long term challenges. Conscience will be the guide and the forces of truth and light will triumph over spiteful and jealous behaviour. Ignorance and oppression will be overcome, goodwill will win over evil intentions.

Negative

This shows that the Questioner, or the relevant person in their environment, is not yet well. It is a warning of continued health problems, or that someone is drained of energy and hope.

There is also the possibility that a struggle will be just too much and that an enemy will gain ascendency over the Questioner. There may have to be a postponement or abandonment of plans soon. There is a lack of courage and resolution and the Questioner is warned that underhanded behaviour will land them in trouble.

XII
THE HANGED MAN

Positive

This card represents a suspension in affairs which will be followed by a turning point in the Questioner's life. However, the changes are most likely to be in *mental attitude* rather than in actual events – although events could conspire to cause this. The general impression is that the Questioner will soon abandon outmoded methods of thought in favour of a more philosophical outlook on life. The effect of this card is often described as taking someone away from materialism towards a more spiritual outlook on life. This concept involves sacrifice in some form or other. A good illustration of this idea carried out to the ultimate, would be that of St Francis of Assisi who gave up a comfortable life for something which seemed to make more sense to him.

This card may show up when a destructive relationship is coming to an end, and it shows the Questioner that, although they may be lonely (i.e. suspended) for a while, it really will be for the best in the long run. If there are financial or other losses, then the Questioner is being told that they will 'grow' in character as a result of dealing with these problems, and that perhaps this is needed in order to make somebody more appreciative of the non-material aspects of life such as love, friendship or self respect. One simple instance of this kind of gradual change in circumstances is when loving parents find that their brood is leaving the nest.

On a practical level this card says that there may be something very good which results from difficult circumstances, such as the Questioner being given the sack from his job, a situation which will require the Questioner to assess his or her abilities and could, when seen in the long run, be very beneficial. There will definitely be some form of hiatus between the former situation and what is yet to come, there must be some sacrifices made, this should be

used constructively so as to create a satisfactory future outlook on life.

Negative
There is not much that *is* negative about this card except that it advises the Questioner to take a philosophical view of any sacrifices that he or she may have to make. It also shows that the Questioner may be longing for change and not able to accept the rather stagnant situation that is going to prevail over the next few months. This card shows the need to grow up and accept that situations are not always of one's own choosing but occasionally have to be endured for a while.

There is a warning against making *useless* sacrifices, or putting up with a poor situation because it is easier and less frightening than taking the risk of making changes. The Questioner should stop banging his or her head against the same old brick wall. Clear

and objective thought is required now, seek guidance, then take
the road which feels right inside.

XIII
DEATH

Positive

This card usually puts the wind up people when it appears in a
spread, but I have *never* known it to mean that the Questioner is
about to die! To be honest, in certain circumstances I *have* seen this
card foretell the death of somebody in the life of the Questioner,
but this is usually no great surprise as the dying person is generally
old and very sick by the time of the reading.

The more usual meaning of this card is *change*. This means that
the Questioner can expect some situation to come to a complete

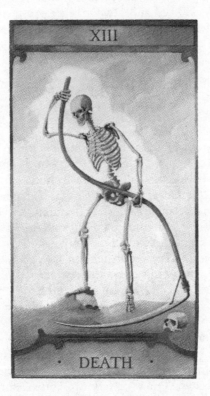

end which clears the way for a fresh start. An apparent misfortune may be a blessing in disguise. There may be death of the old self, inner or outer changes that will lead shortly to a new way of life. On the whole, I would suggest that the events which cause changes are not going to be pleasant to begin with, there may be the loss of a friendship or relationship of long standing. Somebody may leave, there may be financial losses or, in extreme circumstances, the loss of a home or a change in one's health (look at other cards for some sort of indication). However, the meaning here is that there is always a chance to make good. Changes which may be hard to cope with will clear away a certain amount of unnecessary rubbish from the past and leave the Questioner free to make a new start.

Negative

This is really no different from the 'positive' reading except that on the one hand the effects should not be quite so drastic or so out of the blue. There is a warning that this situation should be dealt with in a fairly positive and active manner or a terrible feeling of lethargy and depression might set in. This card also indicates that the Questioner may be stagnating, afraid of losing what he now has.

XIIII
TEMPERANCE

Positive

This is a very pleasant card, it foretells a time of peace and harmony to come. If the Questioner has been going through a rather fraught period, he will soon be feeling calmer and coping better. In fact, the central impression of the Temperance card is of coping well and relaxing. There is harmony here, this may be applied to future relationships, family situations, work, money, health, in fact any aspect of life. The position of this card in a spread will give the Reader an idea of how to interpret this.

The other theme of this card is that of *moderation*. Therefore, if the Questioner has been overdoing anything, be it work or play, good sense and a balanced attitude will apply in the future. There may be a time of frugality when this card appears, this should not be too much of a struggle as it will give the Questioner a chance to make good use of what he already has. There may be some slight material hardships, but spirituality will bring comfort. To my mind this card says, 'Put your feet up, you've done enough'.

Negative
The only negative ideas that this card suggests are that the
Questioner will be too busy in the future to be able to see where
he is really going. There may be continued pressures and anxieties
and the Questioner may find it difficult to cope with all the
separate demands that there are on his or her time. Frankly, the
answer here is to make an assessment of what can be left for
another time and to concentrate on what absolutely must be done.

Intemperance is also a possibility, so if the Questioner is
overdoing the good things of life, the advice is to cut back a bit.

XV
THE DEVIL

Positive
This is the card which upsets people who are religious or are afraid

of Tarot cards in general because we all know that the Devil is evil.
Well, so he is, but the evil can be of our making in that we allow
ourselves to behave stupidly. There is a strong warning here not to
be talked into evil (or even black magic) by dangerous people.
There is also an element of bondage; enslavement to outmoded
ideas possibly, or to a job or house which needs to be left for good.
The most obvious form of slavery comes from being tied to people
who are no good for you. Perhaps it is time to take a realistic look
at current relationships and to stop blaming others without also
looking inwardly. The Devil urges the Questioner to be very
practical, even with essentially non-practical matters.

The Questioner needs to become more independent and to stop
accepting unpleasant situations just for the sake of peace. The
message here is that one will continue to be oppressed unless the
chains are broken. If this card shows up in an area concerned with

money, then it might show that for the time being, the Questioner will be tied to a particular job because he or she cannot afford to do otherwise. Perhaps there is a way out, it is possible to gain qualifications and become trained for something better, even though it might take a long time. It is worth thinking positively and practically about future improvements and changes. Above all, the Devil is a practical lad, not spiritual at all!

This card is also concerned with sexual matters. There are many reasons why sex could present problems, but the message of this card is that sex may well become an important factor in any future decisions. Also that the Questioner may soon be involved in an extremely hot and passionate love affair.

Negative
Frankly, this card is fairly negative whichever way up it is, but the reverse meaning can show that the influence is passing, and that the chains which have held the Questioner are shortly going to be broken. The Questioner is beginning to wake up about the situation and may shortly be able to do something really positive to break out.

This card still warns of becoming involved with evil people and of dirty deeds to come. Follow your conscience, take good advice and when in doubt, keep to the straight and narrow.

XVI
THE TOWER

Positive
This is a most unpleasant card to find in a reading. To be honest, I advise people not to get *too* worried unless it comes up in repeated readings, but whatever way one cares to look at it the Tower brings bad news. There is definitely going to be some sort of loss, even a calamity of some kind. Security, as the Questioner has known it in the past, is going to be destroyed and the troubles are likely to come amazingly quickly when they start. Illusions are going to be shattered and the truth about people and situations will be revealed in startling clarity. There will be a questioning of previously accepted beliefs, trust will be destroyed. There could even be some sort of disgrace.

I am by nature an optimist, but even I cannot find much that is good about this card. At one time I kept getting the Tower in my own readings, and sure enough, our family suffered an appalling financial loss, but we fought our way back to solvency and feel

quite proud of ourselves having done so.

Negative
Negative and positive are not really apt terms for this card; however, to see this card reversed in a spread does seem to show that the problems are here and now rather than in the future. The reversed Tower indicates something in the nature of a long term misery, rather than a sudden catastrophe, although current and future difficulties may be stemming from a sudden disaster in the recent past. Also, the Questioner can now either make strides to overcome difficult circumstances or remain in the midst of them. There is likely to be continued oppression, the problems are not solved yet.

XVII
THE STAR

Positive

This card is truly the 'Star of Hope', and it brings hope, faith and optimism to any part of the spread that it touches. In general, it is a clear indication that things will go well in the future. If the Questioner has been going through a particularly rough patch, then life will soon become smooth again. If there has been a health problem, then this is a wonderful card to see in a reading.

On a more practical note, it is worth taking account of the position of the Star in a spread as its message may apply to a particular area of life. For instance, if applied to career matters, it could show that a problem will soon be solved, past efforts will be appreciated and rewarded. New enterprises or new jobs will go

well, promotion could be on the way and any new venture will flourish. Obviously, this hopeful message can be applied to relationships, exam prospects – even the driving test. If it seems to show up in a relatively unimportant area of the spread, such as a holiday, then it would be telling the Reader that this particular holiday is going to be a good deal more for the Questioner than they imagine.

There is something of an educational slant to this card as it can mean that educational and artistic matters are soon going to be important and that the Questioner would soon be able to make good use of his or her talents. Travel could be on the way, because the general idea of this card is expansion of the horizons and very positive new experiences. It sometimes indicates an increasing and purely beneficial interest in the occult.

Negative
This card does not really have a negative side to it except that it can show some doubts about a new venture, there is a touch of pessimism when the Star is reversed, and perhaps a warning not to expand one's horizons too much just at the moment. It just shows some doubt about the future.

XVIII
THE MOON

Positive
The central theme of this card is one of illusion. This is rather a difficult concept to understand as mystery and illusion can be both good and bad depending on the nature of the Questioner and the area of life that this card affects. Experience has taught me that if this card pops up early on in a Tarot session, then I am dealing with highly charged emotions. If the Questioner has just fallen in love and is not sure how things are going, if a relationship seems to be going nowhere, or working its way to a close, then the Moon will often be one of the first cards to appear. This card clearly shows that everybody concerned in the relationship is muddled, not sure about what they want or where they are going. There could be a good deal of insincerity on both sides. There is no sensible advice that a Reader can hope to give as these kinds of problems defy logic. The Questioner's best hope is to avoid making too many concrete plans and let things float along for a while.

If the Moon card points to other areas of life, such as finances or work, then deception and trickery are definitely in the air. On a

very mundane level, even simple plans can be screwed up when the Moon arrives on the scene, letters will go awry, travel plans will be completely fouled up. Messes, muddles, deception, lies and frustration are on the way for sure, and if there is a woman around who can give the Questioner trouble, she will not hesitate to do so.

On a more positive side, the Moon gives the Questioner a chance to use his or her imagination, and this can be positively channelled into artistic pursuits. There could soon be a development of occult powers. The Questioner would do well to rely on 'gut feelings' in relation to any doubtful situations, as they are going to be far more accurate than reason.

Negative
This card is much the same either way up, but lies and insincerity will definitely be around the Questioner, the muddles and failures

may be of a fairly minor matter, but they will be irritating just the same. Either way up, this annoying card can tease the poor Questioner by showing that the future is yet to be revealed and that the cards are not in the mood to be particularly informative just now.

XVIIII
THE SUN

Positive

This is a lovely card, as it means joy and happiness are on the way. The sun is about to shine on the Questioner and will soon make him feel very good. There is not much to say about this card except that whatever area of the Questioner's life is touched by it will bring happiness and success. If there has been poor health, then there could be no better card to turn up. All efforts will be

rewarded, trials overcome, there will be good friends, comfort and happiness. Marriage will be happy and successful, there will be unselfish love and a great deal of fun and frolic ahead. All proposed enterprises will go well.

I have often seen this card show up shortly before the birth of a child, and if the Questioner is doubtful about the ability to have children, then there could be no better card to find than the Sun. There may be grandchildren soon, or just neighbourhood children, the Questioner may even be working among children, but whatever the connection, there will be joy and fun of a youthful and exhuberant nature.

Negative

This shows that there is *potential* for happiness ahead but that it is rather clouded at the moment. There will be success and achievement, but it may take a bit of time to come along. There will be great improvements but complete satisfaction will take a little longer to achieve.

This card can sometimes be a little sad when associated with children. It may show that a child is shortly to become sick, or that there may be difficulties related to pregnancy or birth. It is even possible, when looked at with other cards in the spread, that a child could prove to be a nuisance in the eyes of the Questioner, or the cause of disagreements. The reversed Sun sometimes shows up when the Questioner decides against having a child and can indicate a forthcoming sterilization, vasectomy or even an abortion (especially if the reversed Empress is also in the spread).

This card also indicates that the Questioner's marriage is not a great success and that he or she is not appreciated.

XX
JUDGEMENT

Positive

This card indicates that a phase is definitely coming to an end. The Questioner will soon be able to look back over what they have been doing and make a clear evaluation of past events. In practical terms, the Judgement card could mean rewards, promotions or even a retirement party with gifts and good wishes for the future. Although this card represents an ending, it is more of a logical conclusion than a wrench, and in any circumstances the Questioner will feel that he has done his duty and now has a clear conscience.

All endings are also beginnings, the end of a project also means the chance to start a new one, and at least the Questioner will start out with the confidence of having accomplished the previous project satisfactorily. There is a feeling of rejuvenation attached to this card, therefore if one has been tied down looking after a sick or demanding relative who is possibly soon to be released from suffering, then the Questioner will feel satisfied that they have done all that could be done and at the same time will also relish the freedom of being able to make a fresh and unfettered start.

There is another far more practical level to this card, and that is of strictly *legal* judgments. If the Questioner is due to have any dealings with the law, then the outcome will be favourable. I suppose it is not surprising but I often find this card turning up when the Questioner is on the point of a divorce as, on the one

hand, it shows the end of the marriage and on the other, the legal settlements which are to come.

Negative
The reversed Judgment card still refers to endings but the feeling is that the Questioner will not be too satisfied with the circumstances surrounding the events. This could mean that the Questioner would know in his heart of hearts that he could have done much better. That could apply to educational matters, work or relationships. The Questioner knows that they could have been a better friend, or just done more for others. There has been a shortsighted and selfish attitude somewhere along the line.

On another level, legal matters are not well starred when this card turns up reversed – especially in any position in a spread which refers specifically to the law.

XXI
THE WORLD

Positive
If the Questioner is nearing the end of a project, then he will soon be able to survey the work done with a sense of pride and accomplishement. This card, like so many of the Major Arcana, is about turning points but in this case a gradual and satisfactory ending with the implicit feeling that new projects soon to be embarked upon will go well too. There is success on the way, there will be praise and reward for satisfactory completion. The Questioner will elicit the admiration of others and will have reason to feel proud. There will be good fortune and above all spiritual enlightenment. The World card shows clearly that the Questioner is about to gain some insight and a sense of inner peace.

On a more mundane level, this card often indicates travel and can even go as far as to suggest emigration because it carries the notion of a new life in a new place. This may just be a move of house, particularly if it is in connection with a change in the Questioner's circumstances, for example, children being born or becoming independent. But in my experience there is more than a hint of foreign places and of new adventures to come.

Negative
The Questioner might display an inability to accept change and an unreasonable desire to stick in a rut, but on the other hand, this could be a good thing as it shows stability and permanence rather than uncertainty and restlessness.

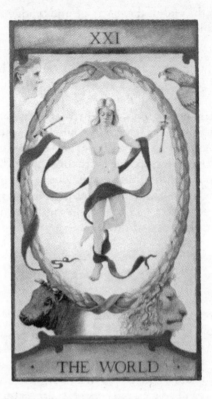

The worst aspect of the negative World is that the Questioner may find himself envious of other people and unsatisfied with his own progress. However, all is not lost even now, there can be fulfilled ambitions and a fair amount of success, but only after a bit of time has passed. Be patient, keep trying, that is the message here.

9
QUICK CLUES TO THE MAJOR ARCANA

O	**The Fool**	Optimistic fresh start. Person lacking depth of knowledge rushing in where angels fear to tread – probably getting away with it. Fun, light-hearted attitude.
I	**The Magician**	New opportunities to use talents. Beginnings in business. Salesmanship and trickery. Boldness, self-reliance, confidence. *Negative:* Could slip-up due to overconfidence or bad judgement.
II	**The High Priestess**	Cool, clever woman. Intuition, sense, a tough-minded attitude. Points out areas of life where the Questioner cannot yet see the whole picture. *Negative:* Lack of sense or intuition.
III	**The Empress**	Pregnancy. Creativity and material abundance. Comfortable life, especially at home. Safety and security. *Negative:* Lack of satisfaction/material goods.

IIII	**The Emperor**	The boss. Kindly authority, father figure. Security, solid gains. Long term success, stability. *Negative:* Person who falls down on the job.
V	**The Hierophant**	Tradition, marriage, stability. Friendship, acts of goodness. Sometimes overkindness. *Negative:* Eccentricity, unconventionality or refusal to change.
VI	**The Lovers**	Love, affection, partnership. Also choices, sticky decisions. Meetings and partings.
VII	**The Chariot**	Work and travel. Having too much to handle. Responsibility. Rush to get everything done. Travelling or doing anything with a purpose.
VIII	**Justice**	Legal matters, fair play, balance.
VIIII	**The Hermit**	Centering oneself, reflection, meditation. A good adviser. Loneliness and withdrawal from life, but sensibly – with a bit of luck.
X	**Wheel of Fortune**	Change, turning point – look to the *area* of the spread for further information. Ups and downs of life.
XI	**Strength**	Health – good and bad. Quiet courage, strength of position in present circumstances. *Negative:* Too much control of self or others.
XII	**The Hanged Man**	Suspension, also sacrifice. Slow dawning of new ways of thinking. Initiation.
XIII	**Death**	Change, endings and beginnings – not easy, but necessary. Sometimes actual death. Loss of a friend or a relationship. *Negative:* Can also mean *slow* change, deciding not to rock the boat if card is reversed, also near-death possible.

XIIII	**Temperance**	Moderation, sensible lifestyle, peace, also coping well. *Negative:* Over-restraint, putting up with too much.
XV	**The Devil**	Bondage, people who are bad for one. Lust, sex – can be fun but motives must be watched. *Negative:* Reversed card can mean release from bondage, new meaning to life. Good sexual relations.
XVI	**The Tower**	Chaos and destruction. Security is shattered, important losses of some kind. Questioner is left with a clear understanding of circumstances that result from unpleasant events.
XVII	**The Star**	Hope, faith, something to look forward to. Also (vaguely) travel, the arts and the occult. *Negative:* If reversed, there could be delays or pessimism.
XVIII	**The Moon**	Romance not going quite right. Emotion, insincerity. Vagueness, untrustworthy people in business around one. Deceptions.
XVIIII	**The Sun**	Confidence, success, happiness, celebrations. Matters relating to children. *Negative:* Family problems, success is sure but delayed or modified.
XX	**Judgement**	End of a job of work, end of a long term situation. Endings not so much with regret, as feelings of having done one's duty. Reward, retirement. *Negative:* Loss, separations, endings.
XXI	**The World**	End of a phase, new one will start soon. A new environment, travel and possibly connections with the occult. Success, approval, hope for the future. *Negative:* Some improvement but also disappointment.

10

SIMPLE SPREADS

Before Spreading the Cards

Shuffle the cards a little, then ask the Questioner to shuffle them well. If the Questioner finds it too hard to shuffle them, then you might suggest that the cards are put face downwards on the table and stirred around, touching as many of them as possible. When the Questioner has finished shuffling (or stirring), ask them to cut the pack into three decks, using the left hand – because it is closest to the heart.

If you wish to give an upright and reversed reading, you may ask the Questioner to point to one of the decks, which you can then turn around. The Questioner should then put all the cards back into one pack, there is no special order for this; and finally the Questioner should put them down on the table. You then take the cards *with the end which was nearest to the Questioner now nearest to you* and you can start to take the cards from the top of the deck for your reading. In the case of a reading which uses only a few cards, you may ask the Questioner to spread them out on the table and to pick out the relevant number of cards for the subsequent reading.

How to Spread the Cards

The first and most vital point to grasp is to get into the habit of turning the cards over from side to side, not from top to bottom. This is so that you do not reverse cards which are upright or put reversed cards up the right way.

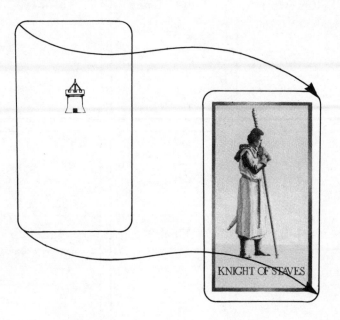

Remember – Turn the cards from side to side.

The Six Card Choose-it-Yourself Spread

The easiest way for a complete beginner to start to read the cards is to make a list on a piece of paper of six areas of life which are of special interest to the Questioner at that particular time. Of course, the Reader may also *be* the Questioner. Then pick out six cards, either from the top of the deck or at random and make up a story based on the cards' meanings. (See page 128ff.)

Once you have grasped this method, go over the six again, either right off the top of the deck or with selected cards and see how the 'story' progresses. Alternatively, choose one or two categories out of the six and put another card or two on top of them to 'zoom in' onto a particularly important area of interest.

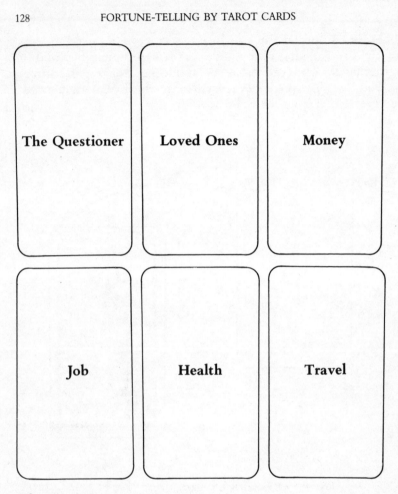

The Questioner

Two of Staves (reversed)
In the case of this reading, there appears to be a break up of a
partnership concerned with business matters. It is possible that
pride on one or both sides was a contributory factor here, also bad
luck or bad timing in business matters.

Loved Ones

Page of Staves
On one level this card tells us that the Questioner has children and
may be worried about one of them. On another level, there is a lot
of correspondence, writing, telephoning, travel and business to be
done by and for the family.

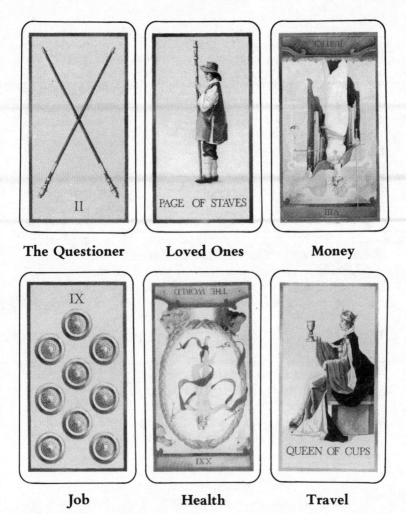

The Questioner	Loved Ones	Money

Job	Health	Travel

Money

Justice (reversed)

This is a Major Arcana card and it is reversed, therefore it points to a major problem in the life of the Questioner at the time of the reading. The Justice card is all about balance and fair play, and with regard to this reading, I would suspect a good deal of worry in this area in the near future. There is even an indication that a legal matter will rear its head and soon cause the Questioner some trouble.

Job

Nine of Coins
This is clearly a good omen, but it shows that work carried out in or near the home is more likely to lead to success (and money) than that which is done away from the home. There is an element of things yet to be revealed, and a feeling that something, probably involving work in or near the home, is likely to turn out well.

Health

The World (reversed)
This card appears to be presenting a major problem for the Questioner. It seems as if health matters are changing the Questioner's life. This may be the Questioner's own health or that of acquaintances. The message here is that the health problems will not go away, and that the changes, although not liked, have to be lived with. One thing is certain, the World that the Questioner has occupied until recently will never be the same again. A deeper reading will show how this will ultimately affect the Questioner.

Travel

Queen of Cups
I chose this category because it is less 'weighty' than the preceding ones. This card clearly indicates that travel will be a pleasurable experience for the Questioner. He or she can expect to meet a fair woman, possibly a foreigner, who will be kind and helpful. There could be fun, good food, laughter and romance connected with travel in the future.

The 'Consequences' Spread

This spread is used by some professional Readers when the Questioner wants to focus on a particular problem. The Reader ought to choose a Significator for this spread (see page 19).

The spread should be interpreted as follows:

1. The Significator.

2. The Questioner, or some clue as to the circumstances surrounding him or her.

3. The background to, or the cause of the problem.

4. The past.

5. The future.

6. Suggestions as to future actions.

7. Environment or persons close to the Questioner.

8. Outcome or consequence of actions.

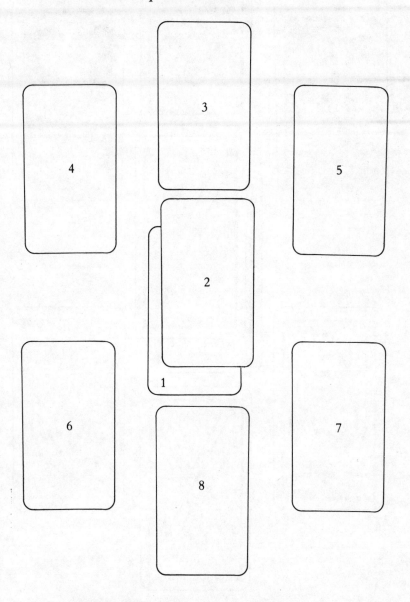

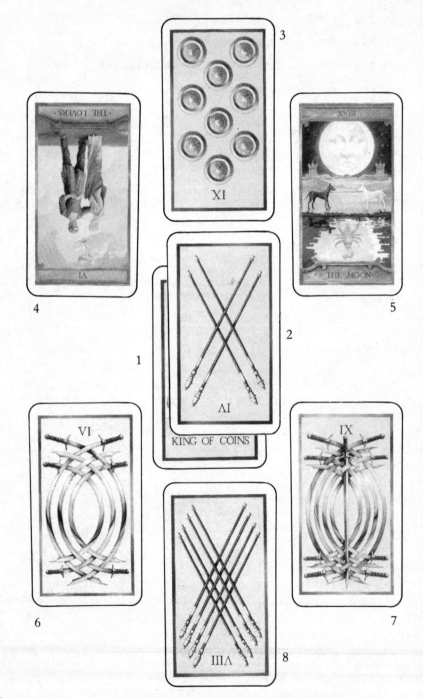

Sample Reading for the 'Consequences' Spread

1. *King of Coins (Significator)*

2. *Four of Staves*
The Questioner is worried about an established business that they own, possibly the cost of the upkeep of the premises is worrying them.

3. *Nine of Coins (reversed)*
Confirms the reading from card number 2. Money and the recession are worrying the Questioner.

4. *The Lovers (reversed)*
Partnership problems, decisions have been made by both partners. This does not seem to have been easy for them.

5. *The Moon*
Some deception to come, problems ahead which cannot be foreseen. Decisions will be made on an emotional basis.

6. *Six of Swords*
Travel will be required in order to secure more business. This may even be overseas travel. There will be a slow improvement, calmer financial waters are on the way.

7. *Nine of Swords*
Other people in the business environment will cause worries and problems, there may be a few sleepless nights for the *partner* of this business.

8. *Eight of Staves (reversed)*
There will be some jealousy or spite coming to the Questioner. The business must not expand too quickly. There could be confusions and problems relating to the *partner's* emotional state and woolly state of mind over the next few months. The overall message is to keep to a steady course and be prepared to become independent of the partner (Six of Swords) if necessary.

SPECIAL PURPOSE SPREADS

The 'Consequences' Spread, Using the Major Arcana Alone
Choose a Significator from the court cards of the Minor Arcana, then spread the cards using just the Major Arcana.

1. *Queen of Cups (Significator)*
This is a fair-haired married woman.

2. *Magician*
The Questioner is coping with life very well now. She is not afraid to take chances and she knows she can rely on her own personality to see her through most things.

3. *The Moon*
Emotional matters cause concern. Her family and close associates worry her. She also has trouble controlling her own emotions at times.

4. *The Hermit*
She has spent time assessing her position in the past and knows what it feels like to be lonely. She has assessed herself and her situation with the benefit of advice from trusted people around her. She knows herself and her abilities well.

5. *The Tower*
The Questioner is in for a shock. There is trouble ahead and this will be dumped into her lap very suddenly.

6. *Strength*
She will have the ability and the courage to deal with the coming problems herself. She may have help from strong or influential friends.

7. *The Priestess*
The Questioner will be able to call on the help of women friends. They will not hand out sickly sentimentality but will be able to give sensible, practical help and advice. She has one friend in particular who is very intuitive, and can be trusted.

8. *Emperor*
This could mean that an influential man will come to the aid of the Questioner. It could just mean that public events will work in her favour. On another level, this would mean that she comes out of any future problems with dignity and without losing any of her present status or possessions.

The Annual Spread
This is a useful spread for those who wish to know when a proposed event is going to take place. It is also good for a general twelve month reading.

The method is simple. Just lay out the cards in the form of a clock and read them month by month, starting with the current month unless the reading is done very near the end of a month, when it would make sense to start from the next month. This can be done with just one card for each month, but two or three cards per month give a fuller, more complex reading.

It is a good idea to take note of the position of any Major Arcana cards, and in particular, any month where two or three Major Arcana cards fall together. This will show the most important times in the year ahead.

This method can be used for the timing of more immediate events, as the twelve card circle can be adapted to show twelve *weeks* ahead, or even twelve *days* ahead. However, it is more usual to use this spread for the coming year.

Sample Reading for the Annual Spread
I have deliberately made the interpretation of this sample reading rather brief in order to simplify what can be a very long reading. It is a good idea to put one extra card right in the middle of the spread, which may give a powerful clue as to the main event of the forthcoming year. I have used all the cards in the upright position for this reading.

One for Luck

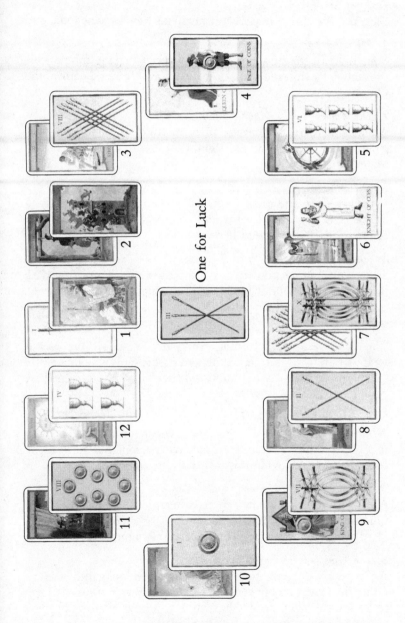

'One for Luck'

Three of Staves
New projects this year, probably involving travel and negotiations.

1. *The Emperor + Ace of Swords*
Something begins now, this should be very satisfying and possibly profitable. Passion and sexual satisfaction *might* enter the life of the Questioner now.

2. *The Tower + The Hanged Man*
A shock involving some sacrifice. A truth of some kind will emerge very clearly. A very significant month as these are both Major Arcana cards.

3. *Strength + Eight of Staves*
Recovery from the previous month's events, bouncing back to health and control of situations. Travel, new horizons, and negotiations are indicated here.

4. *Queen of Swords + Page of Coins*
There could be a problem regarding a youngster and/or a dark haired woman. If not, then this could be a business matter between the Questioner and a woman.

5. *Six of Cups + Wheel of Fortune*
This has got to be a turning point, but somehow the past is wrapped up in all this. Past skills and past friends may be helpful (or harmful) now. Past emotional ties may be reformed or completely broken now.

6. *Knight of Cups + The Hermit*
A fairish man may give the Questioner very good advice. This man may be a rather lonely, introspective person, but he will be friendly or even loving towards the Questioner.

7. *Ten of Staves + Ten of Swords*
A very trying month when there is just too much to do and the Questioner will be carrying the can for other people's failings. Hard work and difficult people mark this month.

8. *The Lovers + Two of Staves*
A temporary or permanent partnership. This looks like business rather than pleasure but could be a bit of both. Decisions will have to be jointly taken now. Alternatively, a love relationship may now begin to include work related matters.

9. *King of Coins + Seven of Swords*
There could be some sort of split up with the Questioner taking part of something that is shared, and leaving some to a man of business. There may be legal forms to sign. The business man could give good advice to the Questioner.

10. *The Star + Ace of Coins*
There are great opportunities to make money now. The future looks very bright and hopeful with regard to business and money matters now. There could even be a win.

11. *The Magician + Eight of Coins*
Definitely something good to do with money, this could be a really good job, promotion or a business matter. Success in all undertakings which involve money and skills, especially new skills.

12. *The Sun + Four of Cups*
Things are going to be very good, but emotionally there will be just a hint of sadness. It looks like a year of success in financial and business matters for the Questioner, but a little sad and lacking in the area of love and romance.

The Question and Answer Spread
Sometimes a Questioner just wants a simple answer to a simple question. It is probably better to use a pendulum rather than Tarot cards for this kind of reading, but it can be done by means of the cards. The simplest way of dealing for this is by using the following steps:

1. Choose a Significator for the Questioner.

2. Ask the Questioner to shuffle the cards, spread them out on the table and choose two cards which will shed some light on the root of the problem.

3. Ask the Questioner to choose three cards for an answer to the problem.

4. Ask the Questioner to choose one more card for a final outcome.

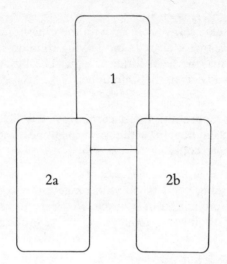

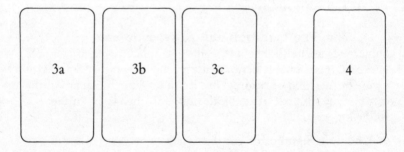

Sample Reading to Answer a Question

Question: Will I pass my driving test?

1. *Page of Staves (Significator)*

2. *Seven of Staves (reversed)* + *Six of Coins*
It appears that the Questioner hates the idea of failing and looking silly as a result. He may be rather worried about the cost involved in taking lessons.

3. (a) *Five of Staves*
There will be a struggle and some setbacks but there is no reason why he should not pass in the end.

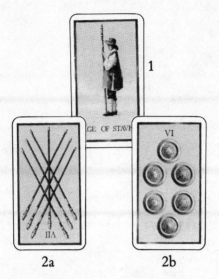

2a   2b

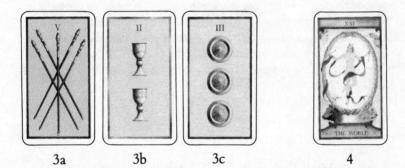

3a   3b   3c   4

(b) *Two of Cups*
Somebody who cares for him will help, possibly by sitting alongside him while he is practising.

(c) *Three of Coins*
This card seems to be jumping the gun as it assumes that the Questioner will be able to cash in on his new found talent.

4. *The World*
Success, completion, new worlds will be available to the Questioner as a result of being able to drive.

12

COMPLICATED SPREADS

The Celtic Cross

This spread is depicted in every book I have ever seen on the Tarot. I personally think it is a confusing spread for a beginner to deal with, but I will show a couple of sample readings for those who would like to be able to use it. It can be done with either the Major Arcana alone or with a mixture of both Arcanas. It is usual to select a Significator from the court cards to represent the Questioner. (See page 19.)

The spread works as follows:

1. The Significator.

2. The Questioner's present situation.

3. Whatever is causing or influencing the situation.

4. The goal, aim or ideal. Alternatively, the best that the Questioner can hope for under the present circumstances.

5. The distant past.

6. The recent past.

7. People or events which will figure in the life of the Questioner in the near future.

8. More information about the Questioner and how he or she affects the surrounding environment.

9. Other people or situations around the Questioner and how *they* affect the Questioner.

10. Inner feelings, hopes and fears.

11. Outcome.

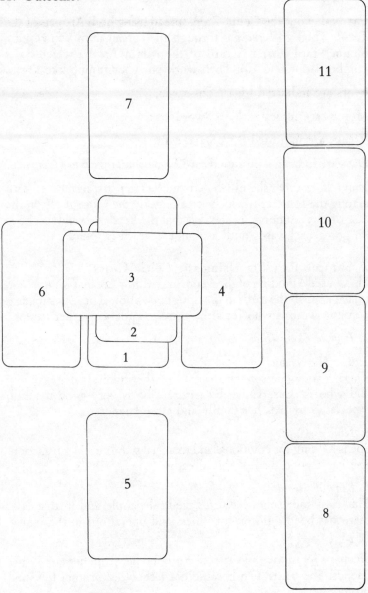

Timing Events, using the Celtic Cross

A friend of mine, Jean Goode, who works under the name of Aquarius, has been a professional Reader for many years. Jean has passed on this unique method of timing events to me for inclusion in this book.

Firstly, lay out the Celtic Cross spread using both Arcanas of the Tarot. Then go *backwards* through the spread until you reach a number card (that is a card of the Minor Arcana which has a number from 1 to 10). Then work out your timing like this:

Years are indicated by a Coin card.

Months are indicated by a Sword card.

Weeks are indicated by a Stave card.

Days are indicated by a Cup card *but only if it is next to a Coin card!*

Jean tells me that she usually encounters her first numbered card among the four cards which are alongside the Cross itself. In the case of this not being so, she says that the Reader should just keep on going backwards until a numbered card is found.

A Sample Reading Using the Celtic Cross

I have used a mixture of the Major and Minor Arcanas for this, and I have kept all the cards in the upright position. The Questioner is a young woman who feels the need to progress in her career.

1. *Page of Coins (Significator)*

2. *The Hierophant*
This is a young person who has had a rather traditional upbringing and who is conservative by nature. She is very good-natured, especially towards her family and close friends.

3. *Nine of Cups*
She is looking for emotional and financial stability and satisfaction. She has a good deal of this already.

4. *King of Swords*
This card sometimes indicates medical people and in this case, there has been a history of illness and operations in the past.

5. *King of Cups*
She has a lot of love and affection around her from her family and friends. She trusts men because her father and brother love and protect her.

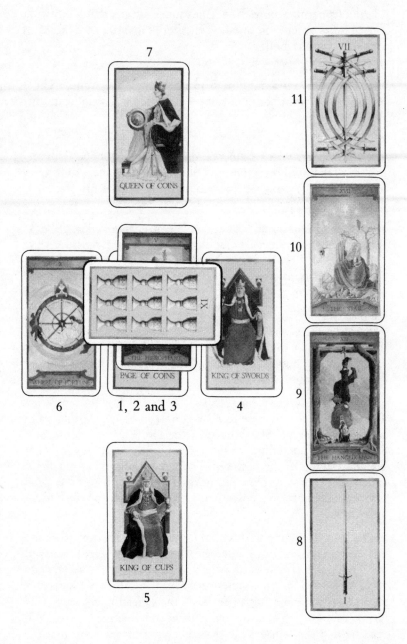

7

QUEEN OF COINS

11

10

6

1, 2 and 3

PAGE OF COINS

4

KING OF SWORDS

9

8

5

KING OF CUPS

6. *Wheel of Fortune*

Change is coming now. The Questioner admits that she would like to improve her job situation and hopes that this card indicates a change for the better.

7. *Queen of Coins*

The Questioner is aiming high in her career, she wants to be a business woman in her own right – the cards so far, indicate that this will happen.

8. *Ace of Swords*

The Questioner wants change and is prepared to cope with any problems that will bring change. She knows that she will have to leave her rather cozy situation and take a chance on life.

9. *The Hanged Man*

Her environment is static. There will be no change unless *she* seeks it herself – she must make the future happen, she must turn her own Wheel of Fortune, no one will do this for her. She will cause other people to make sacrifices for her and she may have to make some herself for the benefit of others.

10. *The Star*

This card is the wish card of the Major Arcana (the Ten of Cups is the wish card in the Minor Arcana) and this area of the Celtic Cross refers to hopes and wishes. It appears that the Questioner can expect to get what she is wishing for.

11. *Seven of Swords (Timing card)*

The Questioner will have to move on in some way, either from her home or her job. She will have to be a little more adventurous. She will leave something of herself behind and will never forget the good things of the past, but she must gather up her resources and make a move within the next year. She will receive good advice (possibly from the King cards in the spread) and she will act upon this.

In fact, I continued with this reading, took another card from the top of the deck and put it over the top of the final card. It turned out to be the Death card which signifies tremendous change coming soon. I also put another card over the Queen of Coins, this turned out to be the Ace of Staves – the Questioner says that she ultimately wants to have her own business. It seems clear from this reading that she will get her desire. This young woman is at the point of changing from being the girlish Page of Coins, to the womanly Queen of Coins. She has very dark hair and is a natural business woman. She likes comfort and stability and a good home and family life.

Jean Goode's Timing Device in Action

This reading was done in December 1983. In August 1984 the Questioner handed in her notice in order to take up a managerial job with much better pay and prospects. This job came her way in July. *This is exactly seven months after the reading was done!*

The Astrological Spread

This spread is extremely popular with professional Tarot Readers because it is so tremendously informative. It does, however, require some basic knowledge of astrology. Most professional Readers are multi-disciplined, which means that they are not only able to use Tarot cards but can also use one or two other methods of divination such as numerology, I Ching, astrology or palmistry. Others have clairvoyant gifts and are able to use psychometry, the crystal, pendulum or inner visions and feelings in order to help them to obtain a successful reading. The non-clairvoyant arts (or sciences) of astrology and numerology lend themselves particularly well to combining with the Tarot.

I am an astrologer and palmist, with some facility for psychometry and healing; therefore I, personally, prefer to blend the Tarot with astrology in order to obtain a really complete reading. There is nothing terribly difficult about this, all that one needs is a handy reference to some of the qualities represented by the astrological houses. However, I must poin. out that the qualities and spheres of life which are associated with the twelve astrological houses do not work in *exactly* the same way for the Tarot. The suggestions which I make here for the twelve positions are based purely upon my experiences with the Tarot and therefore they may diverge a little from pure astrological data.

Position 1

This represents the Questioner. The physical body and what happens to it, therefore it can also represent the general state of health and circumstances. The Questioner's mental and emotional state. Other people who are in the life of the Questioner may show up here in the form of a court card, if so, this shows the one who is most likely to be on the Questioner's mind and how this person is affecting the Questioner. The 1st and 12th positions are probably the most important positions in the spread.

Position 2
This represents money and possessions. Anything of value, including moral values, can show up here. To some extent partners and relationships can show up in this position, but money and goods would be involved somewhere along the line. Matters related to farming, gardening and the land generally show up in this position. Music is indicated here as well.

Position 3
This represents the local environment, matters under negotiation, and in some cases papers to be signed. Local journeys, vehicles and correspondence. People represented by the 3rd position are likely to be those of the same generation or younger, such as brothers and sisters, brothers- and sisters-in-law, neighbours, friends and colleagues, also – although this conflicts with traditional astrology – children and young people. Business matters related to buying and selling seem to come under this position. Education, training and re-training, languages. Some sports and games. Even to some extent the way the Questioner thinks.

Position 4
The home, property and premises of all kinds. Domestic life, roots and background. The parents, especially the mother. Other older females who may stand in place of the mother in some way. Attitudes towards commitment.

Position 5
Children. Fun, holidays, parties, entertainments and gambling. Above all, *lovers*. Creativity, personal projects, the Questioner's own business or other speculative matters. Dancing.

Position 6
Duties and day-to-day service to others. This is usually related to work but may be chores around the home. Superiors and subordinates. Everything related to health, doctors, hospitals, hygiene, etc.

Position 7
Partnerships, relationships, husband, wife. Lovers if the relation-

ship is deep enough. Open enemies. People with whom one must work closely. Business partners.

Position 8
Beginnings and endings. Birth and death. Sexual matters. Money that involves other people, e.g., husbands' or wifes' income, mortgages, taxes, legacies, banking and insurance. Shared feelings, feedback of other people's feelings (especially if they are intense). Crime. The occult. A sense of commitment.

Position 9
Expansion of the Questioner's horizons, e.g., travel, higher education, new environments. Foreigners, foreign goods or business matters, foreign languages. Legal matters, important legal documents and court cases. Religious and mystical matters. The occult (more important in this position than in the 8th). Sporting matters, fresh air pursuits. Gambling on horses. Need for personal freedom.

Position 10
This represents the aims and aspirations of the Questioner. Usually the career, but it may relate to political or creative matters if they are to promote the future success of the Questioner. Parents, especially the father and father-type figures. Status, ambitions, responsibilities and professional standing. How the Questioner is most likely to make a success of his or her career and promote him or herself professionally.

Position 11
This represents social life out in the world. Clubs and societies, friends and acquaintances. Detached relationships and intellectual pursuits. Also hopes and wishes – and the chances of achieving them. Intellectual hobbies. Conversation. Learning for pleasure.

Position 12
The inner thoughts and feelings. Whether the Questioner is his or her own worst enemy, or has inner resources which are not seen or acknowledged by others. An association with hospitals, prisons and asylums may be represented here. This gives a great clue to *inner* strengths, weaknesses and desires. Self-sacrifice, escapism, negative and positive emotions which either give great support to, or tear apart, the Questioner from within. Also *hidden* friends or enemies.

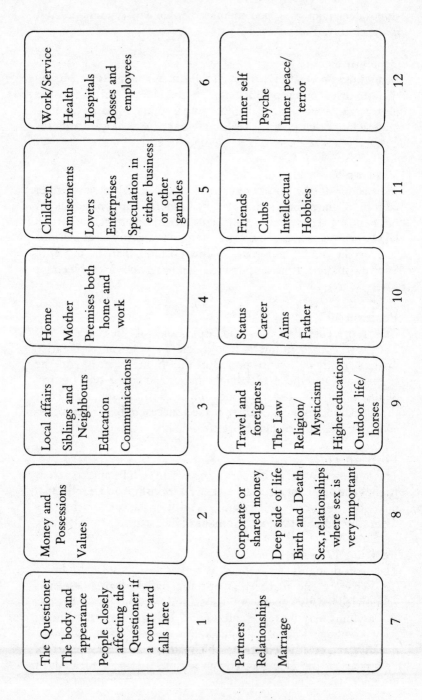

1
The Questioner
The body and appearance
People closely affecting the Questioner if a court card falls here

2
Money and Possessions
Values

3
Local affairs
Siblings and Neighbours
Education
Communications

4
Home
Mother
Premises both home and work

5
Children
Amusements
Lovers
Enterprises
Speculation in either business or other gambles

6
Work/Service
Health
Hospitals
Bosses and employees

7
Partners
Relationships
Marriage

8
Corporate or shared money
Deep side of life
Birth and Death
Sex, relationships where sex is very important

9
Travel and foreigners
The Law
Religion/Mysticism
Higher education
Outdoor life/horses

10
Status
Career
Aims
Father

11
Friends
Clubs
Intellectual
Hobbies

12
Inner self
Psyche
Inner peace/terror

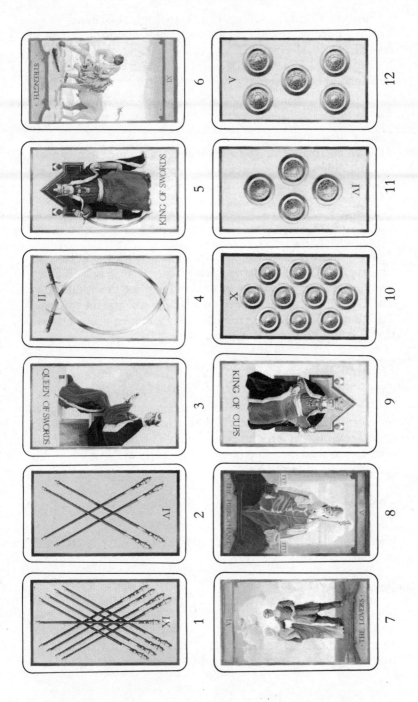

A Sample Reading Using the Astrological Spread

This is a genuine reading for a teenage boy who is just about to take his 'O' level exams and will be leaving school shortly. He is hoping to get a Saturday job soon. He likes girls but has no special girlfriend at the moment.

Position 1

Nine of Staves (reversed)
This young man will soon be leaving a secure and familiar situation. He appears to be rather apprehensive about the future. There is a hint of health problems on the way here too.

Position 2

Four of Staves (reversed)
Again, a feeling that security is threatened. Changes in familiar surroundings will inevitably take place. As this is a 'money' position, he, and his family, may be feeling the pinch just now. This is not really a bad card even if it is reversed, and the feeling is that he will soon become familiar with another environment and that finances will soon pick up as well.

Position 3

Queen of Swords (reversed)
This card seems to show that either someone female around him is going to cause some trouble, or that he is worried about the coming exams. He must be careful with all paperwork and must take care to read the exam questions properly as *that* is where his problems are going to be.

Position 4

Two of Swords
Home life is stable and should not alter much over the next couple of years.

Position 5

King of Swords
This is really strange, because the King card could well represent a medical man and, as it happens, this young man has been complaining about backache and this card falls in the area of the

spread relating to the spine! I think that a visit to our local osteopath (the King of Swords himself no less) in indicated here.

Position 6

Strength (reversed)
This position relates to health. There is quite clearly going to be some problem relating to health in the near future. This seems to stem from a minor back injury from which the young man had suffered recently.

Position 7

The Lovers
Position 7 refers to relationships, and it does not require a 'superbrain' to work it out!

Position 8

The Hierophant (reversed)
He is overgenerous with his time and money, he could well be taken for a ride by an unscrupulous person. He could also find himself in a pre-marital sexual situation within a year or two.

Position 9

King of Cups (reversed)
This could indicate that a foreign man with a fair appearance might cause him some trouble, possibly when he is at college (9th position = further education) next year.

Position 10

Ten of Coins
Whatever happens with his exams or his health problems over the next year or two, he will ultimately do very well indeed. He will have money and a happy family life in the long run.

Position 11

Four of Coins (reversed)
He cannot look to friends to give him much help financially, also he may be disappointed when he finds out just how far his first pay packets go.

Position 12

Five of Coins (reversed)
He feels partly responsible for family money problems in some
way, he would like to help but does not know how to do so just
yet. He feels that any mess he makes of his life at this juncture will
be of his own doing or be caused by people he cannot see and deal
with, rather than his known close associates. His future romance
may be extremely successful but could leave him with some sad
feelings when it comes to its eventual end.

Health by the Cards

The Astrological spread is quite a useful tool for answering
questions about health. The twelve positions point out different
parts of the body. It is quite amazing how the cards will 'pick up' a
health problem, sometimes even before the Questioner realizes he
or she has one. However, I do stress most strongly that the Reader
only mentions the possibility of a health problem and then
suggests that, if the Questioner is worried, they should go to a
doctor. A Reader must never seriously try to diagnose anything.

Position 1

The head, eyes, ears and upper jaw. Also inflammatory conditions
and accidents.

Position 2

The lower jaw, throat, trachea and thyroid.

Position 3

The respiratory system, shoulders, arms and hands. Also the brain,
nervous system and some of the glands.

Position 4

The chest area, breasts, alimentary (food) system, oesophagus,
stomach, gall-bladder and bile ducts.

Position 5

The heart and spine. Also the thymus, the endocrine glands behind
the upper end of the sternum.

Position 6

The lower intestines, colon, bowel, skin, internal and external allergies of a nervous origin. Also general debility and tiredness due to worry or overwork.

Position 7
The kidneys, pancreas and bladder.

Position 8
Gonads, reproductive organs and formation of cells.

Position 9
Liver, pituitary gland, hormone production and physical growth. Also weight problems.

Position 10
The knees, gall-bladder, spleen, skin, teeth and bones. Also ears and bone muscle structure.

Position 11
The lower legs and ankles. Also the circulatory system.

Position 12
The feet, general nervous system and respiratory system. Also allergies (especially to food) and mental problems.

THE prediction

TAROT DECK

The stunningly beautiful Tarot deck used to illustrate this book has been specially designed by Bernard Stringer. It took him two long years to locate an artist — Peter Richardson — who was able to share his inspiration and successfully translate it into images of beauty. The resulting cards are masterpieces of interwoven symbolism and creative artistry.

Included with each deck is a 40 page instruction booklet.

The Prediction Tarot Deck is available from:

U.K.

The Aquarian Press
Denington Estate
WELLINGBOROUGH
Northants
NN8 2RQ

U.S.A.

US Games Systems Inc
38 East 32 Street
NEW YORK
NY 10016

AUSTRALIA

Thomas C Lothian Pty
   Limited
11 Munro Street
Port Melbourne
VICTORIA 3207
Australia

NEW ZEALAND

Thomas C Lothian Pty
   Limited
3/3 Marken Place
Glenfield
AUCKLAND
New Zealand

Of further interest . . .

FORTUNE-TELLING BY RUNES
A Guide to Casting and Interpreting the
Ancient European Rune Stones

David and Julia Line. Casting runes to shed light on the future is one of the least well documented methods of divination, and yet it is one of the easiest, and is remarkable in its accuracy. Here is an essentially practical book, containing all the information needed to cast rune stones and to interpret individual and group meanings from where the stones fall on a runic chart. The authors demonstrate the simplicity of the techniques involved and show that anyone can learn to use the runes to discover the secret of what their future holds.

INDEX